M000189340

THE WAY OF MEN

JACK DONOVAN

[DH]

DISSONANT HUM

UTAH

Copyright ©2012-2022 by Jack Donovan

All rights reserved. No part of this publication may be reproduced, stored in a retrieval system, or transmitted, in any form or by any means, electronic, mechanical, photocopying, recording, or otherwise, without the prior written permission of Jack Donovan.

For current contact information, visit jack-donovan.com.

First edition published in 2012 by Jack Donovan under the Dissonant Hum imprint, in Oregon. This edition published by Brutal Company, LLC.

At the time of this 2022 edition's publication, Brutal Company LLC was located in Salt Lake City, Utah.

FIRST HARDCOVER EDITION

Hardcover ISBN
978-0-578-82400-0

ORIGINAL 2012 PAPERBACK
Paperback ISBN
978-0-9854523-0-8

Library of Congress Control Number: 2022901492

CONTENTS

THE WAY OF
MEN

"...gangsta culture is the essence of patriarchal masculinity."

—bell hooks

PREFACE

I present this book to you without arrogance or hubris.

It is not an advertisement for my own manhood or a boast to flatter the men of my own tribe.

This book is my answer to the question: "What is masculinity?"

If men are a certain way, and there is a way to be manly, then: "What is The Way of Men?"

For decades, people have been talking about a "crisis" of masculinity. Our leaders have created a world in spite of men, a world that refuses to accept who men are and doesn't care what they want. Our world asks men to change "for the better," but offers men less value to them than their fathers and grandfathers had. The voices who speak for the future say that men must abandon their old way and find a new way. But what is that way, and where does it lead?

As I came to understand The Way of Men, I became more concerned about where men are today, and where they are headed. I wondered if there was a way for men to follow their own way into a future that belongs to men.

That's the path of this book. My answers may not be the kind of answers you want to hear, but they are the only answers that satisfied my inquiry.

Jack Donovan

March 2012

Milwaukie, Oregon

THE WAY OF MEN

THE WAY OF MEN IS THE WAY OF THE GANG

When someone tells a man to be a man, they mean that there is a *way* to be a man. A man is not just a thing to be—it is also a way to be, a path to follow, and a way to walk. Some try to make manhood mean everything. Others believe that it means nothing at all. Being good at being a man can't mean everything, but it has always meant something.

Most traditions have viewed masculinity and femininity as complementary opposites. It makes sense to say that masculinity is that which is least feminine and femininity is that which is least masculine, but saying that doesn't tell us much about The Way of Men.

Boys and girls don't pair off at birth and scurry off to a dank cave together. Humans have always been social animals. We live in cooperative groups. Our bodies sort us into groups of males or females. We interact socially as members of one group or the other. These groups aren't arbitrary or cultural—they're basic and biological. Males have to negotiate male and female groups as males. Males aren't simply reacting to females. We react to other males, as males. Who we are has a lot to do with how we see ourselves in relationship to other males, as members of the male group.

A man is not merely a man but a man among men, in a world of men. Being good at being a man has more to do with a man's ability to succeed with men and within groups of men than it does with a man's relationship to any woman or any group of women. When someone tells a man to be a man, they are telling him to be more like other men, more like the majority of men, and ideally more like the men whom other men hold in high regard.

Women believe they can improve men by making masculinity about what women want from men. Men want women to want them, but female approval isn't the only thing men care about. When men compete against each other for status, they are competing for *each other's* approval. The women whom men find most desirable have historically been attracted to—or been claimed by—men who were feared or revered by other men. Female approval has regularly been a consequence of male approval.

Masculinity is about being a man within a group of men. Above all things, **masculinity is about what men want from each other.**

If The Way of Men seems confusing, it is only because there are so many different groups of men who want so many different things from men. Established men of wealth and power have always wanted men to believe that being a man was about duty and obedience, or that manhood could be proved by attaining wealth and power through established channels. Men of religion and ideology have always wanted men to believe that being a man was a spiritual or moral endeavor, and that manhood could be proved through various means of self-mastery, self-denial, self-sacrifice or evangelism. Men who have something to sell have always wanted men to believe that masculinity can be proved or improved by buying it.

In a united tribe with a strong sense of its own identity, there is some harmony between the interests of male groups, and The Way of Men seems straightforward enough. In a complex, cosmopolitan, individualistic, disunited civilization with many thin, *à la carte* identities, The Way of Men is unclear. The ways touted by rich and powerful men are tossed with the ways of gurus and ideologues and jumbled with the macho trinkets of merchants in such a mess that it's easy to see why some say masculinity can mean anything, everything, or nothing at all. Add to that the "improvements" suggested by women, and The Way of Men becomes an unreadable map to a junkyard of ideals.

To understand who men are, what they have in common, and why men struggle to prove their worth to each other, reduce male groups to their nucleic form. Sprawling, complex civilizations made up of millions of people are relatively new to men. For most of their time on this planet, men have organized in small survival bands, set against a hostile environment, competing for women and resources with other bands of men. Understanding the way men react to each other demands an understanding of their most basic social unit. Understanding what men want from each other requires an understanding of what men have most often needed from each other, and a sense of how these needs have shaped masculine psychology.

Relieved of moral pretense and stripped of folk costumes, the raw masculinity that all men know in their gut has to do with being good at being a man within a small, embattled gang of men struggling to survive.

The Way of Men is the way of that gang.

THE PERIMETER

You are part of a small human group fighting to stay alive.

The reason why doesn't matter.

Conquest, war, death, hunger or disease—any of The Horsemen will do.

You could be our primal ancestors, you could be pioneers, you could be stranded in some remote location, you could be survivors of a nuclear holocaust or the zombie apocalypse. Again, it doesn't matter. For humans without access to advanced technology, the scenario plays out more or less the same way.

You have to define your group. You need to define who is in and who is out, and you need to identify potential threats. You need to create and maintain some sort of safe zone around the perimeter of your group. Everyone will have to contribute to the group's survival in some way unless the group agrees to protect and feed someone who can't contribute due to age or illness. For those who can work, you'll need to decide who does what, based on what they are good at, who works well together, and what makes the most practical sense.

Hunting and Fighting

Hunting and fighting are two of the most dangerous jobs you'll need to do to stay alive.

To thrive, humans need protein and fat. You can get enough protein and fat from vegetables, but without an established farm, you're going to be hard-pressed to gather enough vegetables to meet your nutritional needs. A large animal can provide protein and fat for days—longer if you know how to preserve the meat.

The problem with big, protein-rich animals is that they don't want to die. Meat is muscle, and muscle makes animals strong— often stronger than men. Wild beasts come equipped with tusks, antlers, hooves, claws and sharp teeth. They're going to fight for their lives. Taking down a big, protein-rich animal is going to be dangerous. It will require strength, courage, technique, and teamwork. Finding food also requires exploring—venturing out into the unknown—and who knows what lurks *out there?*

If you are going to survive, your group will need protection from predators—animal, human, alien, or undead. If there is someone or something out there who wants what you have and is willing to fight for it, you're going to need to figure out who in your group is going to be willing to fight back. You'll want the people who are best at fighting to stand watch, to defend everything you care about, or to go out and eliminate a potential threat. If someone or something has something that you need, the best way to get it may be to take it. *Who in your group will be willing and able to do that?*

Maybe females are part of your group. Maybe they aren't. If females are with you, they won't have access to reliable birth control. Males and females won't stop having sex, and females will get pregnant. Humans are mammals, and like most mammals, a greater part of the reproductive burden will fall on women. That's not fair, but *nature isn't fair.* Even strong, aggressive women become more vulnerable and less mobile during pregnancy. Even tough women will nurse their young. They'll bond with their offspring and take to caring for them quickly. Babies are helpless, and children are vulnerable for years.

Even if there were no other physical or mental differences between women and men, in a hostile environment the biological realities of human reproduction would still mean that over time more men would be charged with exploring, hunting, fighting, building, and defending. Men would have more time to specialize and develop the necessary skills to excel at those tasks. They wouldn't have a good excuse not to.

Men will never get pregnant, they will never be nursing, and they will be less encumbered by their children. They may not even know who their children are. *Women know who their kids are.* Small children don't depend on their fathers in the same way they depend on their mothers. Men are freer to take risks for the good of the group, believing that their offspring will live on.

As it happens, there *are* biological differences between men and women that have little to do with pregnancy or breastfeeding. On average, men are bigger and stronger than women. Men are more daring, probably more mechanically inclined, and generally better at navigating. Men are hard-   wired for aggressive play. High testosterone men take more risks and seek more thrills. Men are more interested in competing for status, and when they win, their bodies give them a dopamine high and *more testosterone.*[1]

Because your group is struggling to survive, every choice matters. If you give the wrong person the wrong job, that person could die, you could die, another person could die, or you could *all* die. Because of the differences between the sexes, the best person for a job that involves exploring, hunting, fighting, building, or defending is usually going to be a male. This is not some arbitrary cultural prejudice; it is the kind of vital strategic discrimination that will keep your group alive.

Humans, like chimpanzees, will often hunt in teams because cooperative hunting is more effective than hunting alone. When you put together a team—any kind of team—the raw skills of your candidates aren't the only factors you have to consider. You also have to consider the team's social dynamic. Which people will work best together? As a leader, you want to create synergy, reduce distractions, and avoid conflicts within the group. Males will compete for status within any group, but they will also compete for females. Eliminating a second layer of potential jealousy and antagonism may be reason enough to choose a male over a female.

If there are females in your group, they will have plenty of hard and necessary work to do. Everyone will have to pull their own weight, but the hunting and fighting are almost always going to be up to the men. When lives are on the line, people will drop the etiquette of equality and make that decision again and again because it makes the most sense.

That practical division of labor is where the male world begins.

The Party-Gang

Thomas Hobbes wrote that when men live without fear of a common power, they live in a state of "*warre*." In *warre*, every man is against every other man.

Hobbes' idea of *warre* is interesting on a theoretical level, but his warre of all against all is not the state of nature for men. It's natural for a man to look after his own interests, but those interests drive men together—*quickly*. A loner has no one to ask for help, no one to watch his back, no one to guard him when he sleeps. Men have a greater chance of survival together than they do apart. Men have always hunted and fought in small teams. The natural state of warre is an ongoing conflict between small gangs of men.

Chimpanzees organize on a "party-gang" basis, which means they change the size of their groups depending on the circumstances. Chimps gather together in large parties and build alliances for strategic reasons, for mating, and for the sharing of resources. When circumstances change, they break into smaller groups and hunting parties. The smaller groups—the gangs—are the tightest and most stable. The males are loyal and rarely move from gang to gang. Females sometimes join the males in hunting activities, but they are more likely to move from one gang to another over time.

Men tend to organize themselves on a "party-gang" basis, much like chimpanzees.

For example, take military units.

> Army: 80,000 – 200,000 members
> Corps: 20,000 – 45,000 members
> Division: 10,000 – 15,000 members
> Brigade: 3,000 – 5,000 members
> Regiment: 3,000 – 5,000 members
> Battalion: 300 – 1,300 members
> Company: 80 – 225 members
> Platoon: 26 – 55 members
> Section/Patrol/Squad: 8 – 13 members
> Fireteam: 2 – 4 members

All of the men in a given army are part of the same big team, but the strength of the bonds between men will increase as the size of the unit decreases. In smaller groups, men are more loyal to one another.

When writer Sebastian Junger asked US soldiers in Afghanistan about their allegiances, they told him that, "they would unhesitatingly risk their lives for anyone in the platoon or company, but that sentiment dropped off pretty quickly after that. By the time you got to brigade level—three or four thousand men—any sense of common goals or identity was pretty much theoretical."[2] There is frequently rivalry between the groups. Each group has its own regalia, its own traditions, its own symbolism, and a common history.

Some researchers believe that the human brain can only process enough information to maintain meaningful relationships with 150 or so people at any given time.[3] That's about the size of a military company, but also about the size of a typical primitive human tribe, and roughly the number of "friends" most people contact regularly through social networking sites.

Within that tribe of 150, people form even smaller groups. How many people would you loan a lot of money to? How many people could you depend on in an emergency? How many people could depend on you?

If you're like most, that number drops to the size of a platoon, a squad, or even a fireteam. The team size for most group sports is somewhere between the fireteam number and the platoon number. American football teams have around 50 members on a roster, but only 11 are on the field at one time. Baseball teams keep 25 members on their rosters, with 9 on the field. Soccer teams play between 7 and 11 members. Basketball teams play 5. Water polo teams put 7 in the pool.

Men revert back to this archetypal gang size, even for recreation and storytelling. How many main characters are there in your favorite films, books, or television shows? The number works for religion and myth, too. Jesus had 12 apostles. How many Greek gods can you name? Norse?

The group of 2 to 15 men is a comfort zone. It's an effective team size for tactical maneuvers, but it's also socially manageable. You can *really* know about that many guys at one time. You can maintain a good working relationship and a meaningful social history with 100 or so more. Beyond those numbers, connections become extremely superficial, trust breaks down, and more rules and codes—always enforced by the threat of violence—are required to keep men "together." In times of stress—when resources are scarce, when the system of rules and codes breaks down, when there is a lapse in enforcement, or when men have little to lose and more to gain by breaking the law—it is The Way of Men to break off from large parties and operate in small, nimble gangs.

The fireteam-to-platoon-sized gang is the smallest unit of "us." Beyond "us" is "them," and the line that separates *us* from *them* is a circle of trust.

Drawing the Perimeter

The first job of men in dire times has always been to establish and secure "the perimeter."

Imagine yourself again in our survival scenario. People can't fight and hunt and kill all day and all night forever. Humans have to sleep, they have to eat, and they need downtime. You need to create a safe space and set up camp somewhere.

You'll also have to identify some desirable resources, like access to water and food. One of the first things you have to consider is whether the spot makes you vulnerable to attack from predators or unknown groups of men. Then you do some basic recon—you check out the surrounding area to see if there is evidence of another tribe, or undesirable beasts. Tired and satisfied, you and your pals set up a base camp and keep an eye on a rudimentary perimeter.

The survival of your group will depend on your ability to successfully claim land and keep it safe.

When you claim territory and draw a perimeter, that line separates your group from the rest of the world. The people inside the perimeter become *us* and everything known and unknown outside the perimeter becomes *them*.

Beyond the light of your night fire, there is darkness. *They* lie just beyond the flicker of your fire, *out there* in the dark. *They* could be wild animals, zombies, killer robots, or dragons. *They* could also be other men. Men know what men need, and what they want. If your men have something that men want or need, you'll have to be wary of other men. The things that have value to men—tools, food, water, women, livestock, shelter or even good land—will have to be protected from other men who might be desperate enough to harm you to get those things. The perimeter separates men you trust from men you don't trust, or don't know well enough to trust.

People like to make friends. Being on the defensive all the time is stressful. Most people want to trust other people. Most people want to be able to relax. If you are smart, until you know *them*, *they* will remain *out there* on the other side of the perimeter. Even if you let your guard down to cooperate or trade with them, *they* may or may not be absorbed into *us*. As long as other men maintain separate identities, there is always the chance that *they* will choose to put the interests of *their own* ahead of your interests. In hard times, agreements between groups fall apart. Competition creates animosity, and men will dehumanize each other to make the tough decisions necessary for their own group to survive.

If you put males together for a short period of time and give them something to compete for, they will form a team of *us* vs. *them*. This was famously illustrated by Muzafer Sherif's "Robbers

Cave Experiment." Social psychologists separated two groups of boys and forced them to compete. Each group of boys created a sense of *us* based on what they liked about themselves or how they wanted to imagine themselves. They also created negative caricatures of the other group. The groups became hostile toward each other. However, when the researchers gave them a good enough reason to cooperate, the competing gangs were able to put aside their differences and join together in a larger party.

It has always been the job of men to draw the perimeter, to establish a safe space, to separate *us* from *them* and create a circle of trust.

The discovery of new land in the Americas made it possible for men to do this again in recent human history. Small groups of men ventured out into unknown territory because they believed they had more to gain from risk than they could expect to gain through established channels in the old world. They braved the wild, set up camps, and reinvented civilization as the rest of the world looked on. Out there in the dark, there were Injuns, bears, snakes, and other gangs of men willing to use violence to take whatever they wanted. Both the settlers and the natives were men under siege, and they had to harden themselves against external forces. They had to decide who they could trust, who they couldn't, and what they needed from the men around them.

The story of the American West is only one story. How many gangs, families, tribes and nations have been founded by a small group of men who struck out on their own, claimed land, defended it, made it safe and put down roots? If men had never done this, there would not be people living on every continent today.

A Role Apart

You've decided who is in and who is out. You've decided who you trust, and who you don't. You are watching the perimeter, protecting what is inside the circle of flickering light, defending everything that means anything to you and the men who stand with you. It all comes down to you, the guardians, because you know that if you fail at your jobs there can be no human happiness, no family life, no storytelling, no art or music. Your role at the bloody edges of the boundary between *us* and *them* supersedes any role you have within the protected space. Yours is a role apart, and your value to the other men who share that responsibility will be determined by how well you are willing and able to fulfill that role.

Other men will need to know that they can depend on you, because everything matters, and your weakness, fear or incompetence could get any one of them killed or threaten the whole group. Men who are good at this job—men who are good at the job of being men—will earn the respect and trust of the group. Those men will be honored and treated better than men who are disloyal or undependable. The men who deliver victory at the moments of greatest peril will attain the highest status among men. They will be treated like heroes, and other men— especially young men—will emulate them.

In a complex society, almost all of us live deep within the perimeter. We create our own circles and cliques, and we defend them metaphorically. We include people or exclude them for all kinds of reasons. Far from any boundary between threat and safety, people celebrate qualities that have almost nothing to do with survival. The flock bleats for singers, designers, smooth talkers, and people whose only talents are being witty or pretty. The shepherds drive them round to more of the same.

When men evaluate each other *as men*, they still look for the same virtues that they'd need to keep the perimeter. Men respond to and admire the qualities that would make men useful and dependable in an emergency. Men have always had a role apart, and they still judge one another according to the demands of that role as a guardian in a gang struggling for survival against encroaching doom. Everything that is specifically about being a man—not merely a person—has to do with that role.

As you stand back to back, fending off incoming oblivion, what do you need from the men in your group? As you close a circle tighter around dangerous game that could feed you all for a week, what kind of men do you want at your flank?

THE TACTICAL VIRTUES

"*Vir*" is the Latin word for "man." The word "virtue" comes from the Latin "*virtus*." To the early Romans, *virtus* meant manliness, and manliness meant martial valor.[4] Demonstrating virtus meant showing strength and courage and loyalty to the tribe while attacking or defending against the enemies of Rome.[5]

As the Romans became more successful and their civilization became more complex, it was no longer necessary for all men to hunt or fight. The fighting happened at the edge of the perimeter, and the fighting edge of Roman civilization moved outward. For men deep inside the circle, manliness became increasingly metaphorical.[6] Men who did other work could satisfy their need to be seen as men among men by fighting metaphorically, showing social courage, mastering their desires, and behaving ethically. The meaning of the word virtus and the Roman idea of manliness expanded to include values that were not merely survival virtues, but also civic and moral virtues.

Definitions of manliness expand to include other virtues as civilizations grow. However, these other virtues are less specific to men than the fighting virtues, and they vary more from culture to culture. "Civilized" virtue is about being a good person, a good citizen, a good member of a particular society. Manly virtues should be virtues directly related to manhood. The virtues that men all over the world recognize as manly virtues are the fighting virtues. Epics and action movies translate well because they appeal to something basic to the male condition—a desire to struggle and win, to fight for something, to fight for survival, to demonstrate your worthiness to other men.

The virtues associated specifically with being a man outline a rugged philosophy of living—a way to be that is also a strategy for prevailing in dire and dangerous times. The Way of Men is a tactical ethos.

If you are fighting to stay alive and you are surrounded by potential threats, what do you need from the men fighting with you?

What do you need from *us* to fend off *them*?

If eating means facing danger together, who do you want to take with you?

What virtues do you need to cultivate in yourself and the men around you to be successful at the job of hunting and fighting?

When your life and the lives of people who you care about depend on it, you'll need the men around you to be as strong as they can be. Living without the aid of advanced technology requires strong backs and elbow grease. You'll need strong men to fight off other strong men.

You won't want the men in your gang to be reckless, but you'll need them to be courageous when it matters. A man who runs when the group needs him to fight could put all of your lives in jeopardy.

You'll want men who are competent, who can get the job done.

Who wants to be surrounded by morons and fuck-ups? The men who hunt and fight will have to demonstrate mastery of the skills your group uses to hunt and fight. A little inventiveness couldn't hurt, either.

You'll also need your men to commit. You will want to know that the men beside you are *us* and not *them*. You'll need to be able to count on them in times of crisis. You want guys who have your back. Men who don't care about what the other men think of them aren't dependable or trustworthy. If you're smart, you will want the other men to prove they are committed to the team. You'll want them to show that they care about their reputation within the gang, and you'll want them to show that they care about your gang's reputation with other gangs.

Strength, Courage, Mastery, and Honor

These are the practical virtues of men who must rely on one another in a worst-case scenario. Strength, Courage, Mastery, and Honor are simple, functional virtues. They are the virtues of men who must answer to their brothers first, whether their brothers are good or unscrupulous men. These tactical virtues point to triumph. They are amoral, but not immoral. Their morality is primal and it lives in a closed circle. The tactical virtues are unconcerned with abstract moral questions of universal right or wrong. What is right is what wins, and what is wrong is what loses, because losing is death and the end of everything that matters.

Strength, Courage, Mastery, and Honor are the virtues that protect the perimeter; they are the virtues that save us. These are the virtues that men need to protect their interests, but also the virtues they must develop to go after what they want. They are the virtues of the defender and the attacker. Strength, Courage, Mastery, and Honor belong to no one god, though many gods claim them. Whatever men fight for, Strength, Courage, Mastery, and Honor are what they must demand of each other if they are going to win.

Strength, Courage, Mastery, and Honor are the alpha virtues of men all over the world. They are the fundamental virtues of men because without them, no "higher" virtues can be entertained. You need to be alive to philosophize. You can add to these virtues and you can create rules and moral codes to govern them, but if you remove them from the equation altogether, you aren't just leaving behind the virtues that are specific to men; you are abandoning the virtues that make civilization possible.

The men who are strong, courageous, competent and loyal will be respected and honored as valuable members of team "us."

Men who are exceptionally weak or fearful can't be counted on. Men who are inept in some important way must either find a way to compensate—and they will try if they are loyal and honorable, if they *want* to help with the hunting and fighting—or find other work to do in the tribe. A man of questionable loyalty, who doesn't seem to care what the other men think of him or how their tribe is perceived, will not be trusted by the hunting and fighting gang. Men who are not up to the job of fulfilling the first role of men for one or all of these reasons will be pushed out of the hunting and fighting group and sent to work with the women, the children, the sick and the elderly.

Men have different drives, aptitudes and temperaments. Most men have the ability to adapt to the hunting and fighting role, to life at the edge of the perimeter, but some men won't be able to cut it. They will be regarded as less manly and thought of as lesser men. Some men are going to get their feelings hurt. That's not fair, but *fairness is a luxury* that men can ill afford in dire times.

Men who want to avoid being rejected by the gang will work hard and compete with each other to gain the respect of the male gang. Men who are stronger, more courageous and more competent by nature will compete with each other for higher status within that group. As long as there is something to be gained by achieving a higher position within the gang—whether it is greater control, greater access to resources or just peer esteem and the comfort of being higher in the hierarchy than the guys at the bottom—men will compete against each other for a higher position. However, because humans are cooperative hunters, the party-gang principle scales down to the individual level. Just as groups of men will compete against each other but unite if they believe more can be gained through cooperation, individual men will compete within a gang when there is no major external threat but then put aside their differences for the good of the group. Men aren't wired to fight *or* cooperate; they are wired to fight *and* cooperate.

Understanding this ability to perceive and prioritize different levels of conflict is essential to understanding The Way of Men and the four tactical virtues. Men will constantly shift gears from in-group competition to competition between groups, or competition against an external threat.

It is good to be stronger than other men within your gang, but it is also important for your gang to be stronger than another gang. Men will challenge their comrades and test each other's courage, but in many ways, this intragroup challenging prepares men to face intergroup competition. Just as it is important for men to show their peers they won't be pushed around, the survival of a group can depend on whether or not they are willing to push back against other groups to protect their own interests. Men love to show off new skills and find ways to best their pals, but mastery of many of the same skills will be crucial in battles with nature and other men. The sports and games men play most demand the kind of strategic thinking and/or physical virtuosity that would be required in a survival struggle. A man's reputation may keep men in his group from messing with him, and a group's reputation may make its enemies think twice about creating animosity.

Sociologists and street gang experts typically write about an excessive concern with reputation or a desire to avenge "disses" with confused, haughty contempt. But the truth is that men have behaved this way for most of human history, and the strategic reasons why should be obvious to anyone who doesn't feel he can rely on police protection. If no one is coming to save you, you'd better be tough or look tough, and you'll probably want some tough guys ready and willing to get your back.

I have no idea how people manage to be confused about something that simple and obvious, but I'm pretty sure our ancestors would have killed them and taken their stuff.

* * *

The next four chapters will elaborate on what I mean by Strength, Courage, Mastery and Honor. These simple words have many meanings, and they mean different things to different people. The manly virtues represent concepts so universally appealing that even the weak, cowardly, inept, and dishonorable struggle to find ways in which they too can feel that they embody these virtues. With each of the four, I will show why they relate specifically to men, how women fit into the picture, and how the virtues relate to each other. Some of the virtues also have multiple aspects worth parsing out.

After we have examined each of the tactical virtues and considered them amorally, I'll address issues of morality and ethics again, and explain what I think the difference is between being a good man and being good at being a man—and why they're not the same thing.

STRENGTH

If you take a thing apart or modify it, there are certain aspects which must remain intact or be replaced for it to retain its identity. Without certain parts, it becomes something else.

Without strength, masculinity becomes something else—a different concept.

Strength is not an arbitrary value assigned to men by human cultures. Increased strength is one of the fundamental biological differences between males and females. Aside from basic reproductive plumbing, greater strength is one of the most prominent, historically consequential and consistently measurable physical differences between males and females.

It is fashionable today to put the word "weaker" in quotations to avoid offending women when they are referred to as the "weaker" sex. Quotation marks will not alter the basic human truth that men are still, on average, significantly physically stronger than women. Serious people should be able to admit that something is generally true when it is a verifiable fact. There is no good reason to be coy about it.

Strength isn't the only quality that matters. Sometimes it doesn't matter at all. Strength is rarely a disadvantage. However, in our mechanically-assisted modern world, physical strength is often less consequential than it used to be. Of consequence or not, it is what it is.

Women can demonstrate strength, but strength is a quality that defines masculinity. Greater strength *differentiates* men from women. Weak men are regarded as less manly, but no one really cares or notices if a woman is physically weaker than her peers. In a way, this is truer—or truer across classes—than it ever has been. Women living on farms (or in primitive hunter-gatherer societies) were expected to do far more demanding physical labor than any work required of the average woman today.

We admire strength in female athletes, but a beautiful woman who can't lift a bag of groceries will still have many admirers, and plenty of men will be willing to help carry her groceries. Many female celebrities considered beautiful by both men and women are so thin that they look starved and brittle. Collectively, we don't care whether a woman is strong or not. A woman is not considered less womanly if she is physically weak.

Many may consider a woman less womanly if she is too strong. Specifically, a woman tends to look more like a man if she has a conspicuously high level of muscle mass and unusually low body fat. Precisely because of the physiological differences between males and females, only the most dedicated and disciplined female bodybuilders ever manage to look like He-Man action figures with Barbie doll heads. Average women who train with weights will increase strength and overall health, but most will still look like women. Testosterone may or may not play an important role in female muscular development.[7] However, in men, testosterone—the most recognized androgen—has a complementary relationship with increased strength and muscle mass. Men who have more muscle tend to have and maintain higher testosterone levels, and men who have higher testosterone levels tend to have an easier time getting bigger and stronger. Men who increase their testosterone levels—either through training and diet or via artificial means—tend to look *more* masculine. Put differently, men with more muscle look less like most women, and more like the least androgynous men. This has absolutely nothing to do with culture. There is no human culture where men who are weak are considered manlier while women who are more muscular are considered more womanly. The importance of strength varies from society to society (usually in some relationship to available technologies and the kind of work that is required of average people), but strength has been a masculinity-defining quality always and everywhere.

If we are making an honest attempt to understand and define masculinity or manliness[8] as that which pertains to or is characteristic of men, physical strength must figure prominently in that definition. The Way of Men is the Way of the Strong—or at least the *stronger*.

As I and many others have mentioned, strength is not always a great advantage in the modern world. However, if we go back to our primal gang—our band of brothers fighting for survival—the value of strength to the group increases substantially. Where there is work and fighting to be done, the advantages of being stronger are obvious. A man who can hit twice as hard is also, other variables aside, worth more to the gang. In addition to giving a man the ability to take a position of greater prominence in a gang, strength made him more valuable overall. A man who can carry twice as much as another man, other variables aside, is worth more to the gang.

One evolutionary biologist recently suggested that humans stood up because standing up gave human males a greater mechanical advantage when clobbering each other.[9] They may have started walking upright for other reasons as well. On a long enough timeline, "both A and B" is a reasonable explanation, if both explanations are reasonable. As a natural advantage, pummeling power matters. It is also generally believed that fighting is one of the reasons why males have greater upper body strength than females. In the primal gang, the man who is substantially stronger than all of his peers is a juggernaut capable of crushing everyone in his path. He is capable of exerting his will in any way he sees fit. (The will itself is our second manly virtue.)

Strength, in the strictest physical sense, is the muscular ability to exert pressure.

Putting aside the workings of involuntary muscles, for conscious beings strength is the ability to exert force in accordance with one's will. This can be as simple as forcing one bone toward another and releasing it. A certain amount of strength is required to wiggle your finger.

Strength is an aptitude. Strength is an ability that can be developed, but as with intelligence, most people will have a certain natural range of potential beyond which they will be unable to progress. Some individuals will have a greater aptitude for developing strength than others. Humans are unequal in their aptitudes. This is one of the cruel but fundamental truths of human life.

It takes a certain amount of strength to reach for a piece of fruit and yank it away from a plant. Strength is required to build and to farm and to hunt and to carry groceries from the store and put them in your car. Ask an old person if loss of strength has impacted their lives in a negative or positive way. A weaker person is more vulnerable. Less strength means it is less likely that you will be able to push someone away who wants to take something from you, and on a strictly physical level, reduced strength means a diminished ability to take what you want from someone else. A person who is too weak simply cannot survive. It is strength that makes all other values possible.

Strength is the ability to exert one's will over oneself, over nature and over other people.

As we move from the dire circumstances of the survival gang to a luxurious life in a civilized society, the concept of strength doesn't change so much as it expands and becomes a metaphor. The word strength can describe a wide range of abilities and powers without losing its primal meaning or cachet. Strength is the corporeal equivalent of power. Strength is having 300 tanks to use against your enemy's 200 tanks. Strength is the arsenal, but no guarantee that the arsenal will be used. Strength, in this broader sense, is a desirable commodity. Getting stronger—increasing strength—means increasing your ability, as an individual, a gang or a nation, to do as you wish with relative impunity. What is freedom, if not the ability to do what one wishes?

Strength is the ability to move, and greater strength moves more. However, just as muscles can make isometric contractions, strength can also be the ability to stand against outside pressure. Strength is also the ability to HOLD FAST—a tattoo once found on the knuckles of sailors whose lives (and the lives of the gang of men on their ship) depended on their ability to hold on and weather a storm. That strength means both the ability to move and the ability to become immovable is no more a contradiction than the mechanics of a muscle are a contradiction.

Physical strength is the defining metaphor of manhood because strength is a defining characteristic of men. An increased aptitude for physical strength differentiates most males from most women, and this difference, though less important in times of safety and plenty, has defined the role of men for all of human history.

Strength can be put to a variety of uses, but when it is put to no use, it is like a powerful engine collecting dust in a garage or a beautiful singing voice that no one ever hears. A sports car that never puts rubber to the road is just a pretty hunk of metal. To experience the joy of his natural talent, a singer must sing. The experience of being male is the experience of having greater strength, and strength must be exercised and demonstrated to be of any worth. When men will not or cannot exercise their strength or put it to use, strength is decorative and worthless.

COURAGE

Strength is a straightforward, physical concept.

Courage has many names, and has been defined in many ways.

Strength is the ability to move or stand against external forces. Courage is kinetic. Courage initiates movement, action or fortitude. Courage exercises strength. The "cowardly lion"—the tough-looking guy who stands aside as weaker men fight the fight, take the risks and do the work— is worth less than the men who step into the arena.

I will not claim that all exertions of will are courageous, but all acts which require courage are exertions of will. It does not take courage to use strength to pick up a glass and lift it to your mouth. Courage implies a risk. It implies a potential for failure or the presence of danger. Courage is measured against danger— the greater the danger, the greater the courage. Running into a burning building beats telling off your boss. Telling off your boss is more courageous than writing a really mean anonymous note. Acts without meaningful consequences require little courage.

Aristotle believed that courage was concerned with fear, and that while there were many things to fear in life, death was the most fearful thing of all. In his *Nicomachean Ethics*, the brave man is a man who, "is fearless in the face of a noble death, and all of the emergencies that involve death; and the emergencies of war are in the highest degree of this kind." He also made the point that men who are forced to fight are less courageous than those who demonstrate courage in battle of their own free will. Aristotle framed courage as a moral virtue, as a will to noble action. He questioned the courage of those who are confident due to success in battle, though I wonder how such success can be earned, except through some initial show of courage. While it is true that the chests of strong and experienced men often swell when threats are minor, and such men have been known to back down in the face of a legitimate challenge, a certain amount of courage is the product of a successful track record. Is a man who has never won a fight more courageous for taking on an experienced fighter—no matter how noble the cause—or is he simply a fool? Aristotle's mean of courage is not the wild, "rash" confidence of a passionate man who fights in the heat of the moment out of fear or anger. Rather, he suggests that "brave men act for honor's sake, but passion aids them." He does allow that men who act from strength of feeling possess "something akin to courage." [10] Aristotle's formulation of courage, while admirable, is so conditional and lashed to a slippery, high-minded ideal of noble action that trying to determine who is truly courageous becomes a bit of a game.

Andreia, the word Aristotle used for courage, was also synonymous with manliness in ancient Greece. *Andreia* is derived from "andros," which connotes "male" or "masculine." In his book *Roman Manliness*, classicist Myles McDowell argued that the word virtus,[11] which "struck the ear of an ancient Roman much as 'manliness' does that of an English speaker,"[12] meant courage—specifically in battle—in pre-Classical Latin. The word *vir* meant "man," and the *virtus* meant courage.[13] McDonnell wrote:

> "In military contexts *virtus* can denote the kind of courage
> required to defend the homeland, but more often it designates
> aggressive conduct in battle. In non-military situations
> courageous *virtus* usually refers to the capacity to face and
> endure pain and death."[14]

Courageous manliness is personified in the story of Gaius Mucius,
a noble Roman youth from the early Republic. An Etruscan king
named Porsenna had besieged Rome by garrisoning his soldiers
around the city. Gaius Mucius asked the Roman senators for
permission to slip into the Etruscan camp and kill Porsenna. He
killed Porsenna's secretary by mistake, and he was captured by
the king's bodyguards. Gaius Mucius said to the king:

> "I am Gaius Mucius, a citizen of Rome. I came here as an
> enemy to kill my enemy, and I am as ready to die as I am to
> kill. We Romans act bravely and, when adversity strikes,
> we suffer bravely. Nor am I the only one who feels this way;
> behind me stands a line of those who seek the same honour."[15]

Porsenna threatened to throw Gaius Mucius into the fire. Gaius
Mucius responded by thrusting his own hand into the fire. As his
hand burned, he said:

> "Look upon me and realize what a paltry thing the body is for
> those who seek great glory."[16]

Porsenna told Gaius Mucius that, were he a member of his own
tribe, he would commend him for his bravery. Gaius Mucius was
released, but he told Porsenna that there were three hundred
other Romans who would be willing to sacrifice themselves as
he had to save their city, and that if the siege of Rome persisted,
sooner or later one of them would manage to succeed in killing
the king. Porsenna sent an envoy to the Romans, offering peace

terms. Gaius Mucius earned the nickname "Scaevola," meaning "left-handed," after losing his right hand to the fire.

For both Aristotle and the Romans, courage—and manliness— was the will to heroically risk life and limb against a danger to the people of one's own tribe, especially in the context of war with another tribe. Aristotle's most noble form of courage was a willingness to take a necessary risk to ensure the survival of the group. A demonstration of the willingness to risk one's own being for the gang proves loyalty and increases a man's value to the gang. When the chips are down, a man who shows this kind of courage can be counted on to give everything he has—even sacrificing himself—for the survival of the group. When a group is not facing a survival challenge, that group can afford to be metaphorical about courage and acknowledge lesser sacrifices. Until security is established, though, no group can afford to bother with niceties like "intellectual courage."

The word courage is used cheaply today. Any celebrity who gets sick and doesn't spend every day crying about it is lauded by tabloids for his or her "courageous battle" with cancer or chronic fatigue syndrome or depression or even "food addiction." There is nothing wrong with acknowledging the difficulties others face, but we can also acknowledge, as Aristotle and the Romans did, that courage in its highest and purest form involves the willful risk of bodily harm or death for the good of the group. Lesser risks require greater dilutions of courage.

Aristotle believed that heroic courage was the noblest form of moral courage, but he also noted that passion or spiritedness was "something akin to courage." In Plato's *Republic*, it is suggested that savage cruelty comes from the same part of man that inspires acts of great courage.[17] Courage was a trained, mature, socially aware and cooperative form of spirit. Translator Allan Bloom identified the raw form of courage—thumos[18] or "spiritedness"— as "the principle or seat of anger or rage."[19] Socrates likened the guardians of his city to "noble puppies," who would be gentle with the people they knew but be eager to fight ferociously against strangers and outsiders when necessary.[20]

To get at the essence of what masculinity really is, let's remove the gilding of morality and nobility for a moment. While I do believe that some men demonstrate heroic tendencies at an almost instinctive level—like noble puppies—I will also say that before a man can be willing to take a risk for the group, he must be willing to take risks generally. Some men and women are described as being "risk-averse," and will go out of their way to avoid almost any kind of risk at all. Before we can have a willingness to take risks for the group—call that "high courage"—we must also possess some kind of "low courage" that amounts to a comfort with risk-taking. Risk-taking comes more naturally to some than to others, and it comes more naturally to men than it does to women.[21] As strength is trainable, so is courage. But like strength, some have a greater aptitude for risk-taking than others. Males socialize each other—hell, they *taunt* and *goad* each other gleefully—into taking risks. When there is no heroic objective in sight, boys will dare each other to do all sorts of stupid things. However, a male who is comfortable with low risk-taking is likely going to be surer of himself—and more successful—when the time comes to take a heroic risk.

When answering the question "what is masculinity?" it is also important to keep sight of the individual within the group. Heroic courage benefits the group, but as we have discussed, there are benefits to gaining status within the group, and men will fight for that status. This requires a less noble kind of courage. It requires a spiritedness on one's own behalf. The strength of man is not merely a tool to be used in the service of others. Men also use strength to advance their own interests and it is foolish to expect them to make endless sacrifices without personal gain of some kind, be it material or spiritual. We should expect men to fight for themselves, to compete with one another and to look after their own interests. Nothing could be more natural than a man who wants to triumph and prosper.

It is not the strongest man who will necessarily lead; it is the man who *takes* the lead who will lead. This intragroup courage is required for a man to assert his interests over the interests of other men within the group. At the most primal level, asserting your interests over the interests of another man requires a potential threat of violence. This is how men have always sized each other up, and this is how they size each other up today. This base, amoral courageous spirit is required to move ahead of other men within a hierarchy. It's the essence of competitive spirit. Nose-to-nose, men still look each other over and try to perceive whether—and to what extent—another man would be willing to press his interests.

If I push, will he give way? Will he push back?

This basic "push" is the spark of courage. If it isn't sufficiently present in a man, I doubt higher forms of courage would even be possible. There are many names for the kind of courage required to take risks to advance one's own interests. Most people would call it *balls*.

Another word is "gameness." Sam Sheridan wrote about it in *A Fighter's Heart*. Gameness is a term used in dogfighting to describe, "the eagerness to get into the fight, the berserker rage, and then the absolute commitment to the fight in the face of pain, of disfigurement, until death."

In dogfighting, two dogs will fight until they are broken up for some reason. The dogs will be pulled back behind "scratch lines" in their corners and released. Dogs who jump back into the fight—this is called "making scratch"—are said to be "game." Dogfighting is a test of this gameness. According to Sheridan, dogfighting is not meant to be a fight to the death. The dogs fight until one of them refuses to cross the scratch lines and continue the fight.[22] It's like tapping out or saying "uncle."

Men evaluate each other for gameness, and this is the reason it was relevant in Sheridan's book about amateur and professional fighting. This indomitable spirit is a major theme in every heroic journey. In sports, it's part of the comeback tale. A guy faces his toughest challenge, and then, when all but a few have counted him out, he comes back—running on pure "heart"—and triumphs over his opponent. It's the climax of every Rocky story, and it was a gimmick in most of Hulk Hogan's professional wrestling matches. In every *Die Hard* movie, John McClane manages to save the day only after he's been beaten and bruised and comes back from the brink of defeat. These heroes have a push inside that keeps them coming back again and again after others would have given up.

A man who is obviously game can step ahead of a man who is not, simply because he can expect the man who is less game to yield to him. Some people talk about masculinity by attempting to determine who is "alpha" and who is "beta" in a given situation.[23] A friend put it to me this way: "If you can treat another man like he is your kid brother, you are the alpha." The alpha will be the man with more push, and he will push ahead of the beta.

Feigning gameness can be an effective strategy, so long as no one calls your bluff. Gameness can be feigned through body language, through vocal inflection and through word choice. Creating a sense that you are ready to push as hard as necessary to get what you want is a way to establish authority, whether you are a prisoner, a businessman, a law enforcement professional, a parent or someone trying to discipline a dog. Most people will not test someone who is feigning gameness if the actor is convincing enough. Feigning gameness is a means of asserting one's will, and people do it all the time, even in primitive societies. Failed attempts to feign gameness—trying to look tougher than you are, and not pulling it off—are what feminists point to when they talk about "performing masculinity" or putting on a "tough guise." What they are recognizing is the fact that men today still go through the ritual of establishing hierarchies and sizing each other up, even though most are untested and few will ever fight. It can seem silly to watch precisely because it is divorced from the deadly serious tactical reality of a survival scenario.

Feigning gameness can also, unfortunately, lead to delusional behavior. Many people affect the attitudes and postures of violence even though they have no experience with or expectation of physical violence. There is a fearlessness that comes with knowing you can say whatever you want because there is a large, heavily armed man standing behind you. People can talk tough without having to do the primitive math of violence, because they believe that law enforcement will either intervene and stop or punish an attacker. Delusional gameness relies on the deterrent of men and women who are prepared to use violence to enforce the law. Delusional gameness is only possible when there is almost no danger of violent escalation. In less secure, less luxurious times and places, assertiveness must be accompanied by physical courage and daring. When there is no expectation that you will be "saved" or that most people fear the violent retribution of the state, it is foolish to provoke a dangerous-looking man unless you are prepared to fight him.

The raw courage of gameness may correlate with the surety of greater size and strength to some degree, but many smaller men are as game as or more game than their larger counterparts. Flyweight fighters are a good example of men who are extremely game, though they are far less strong than many larger men who are less game. Weight-classed combat sports show that men of all sizes can demonstrate terrific gameness.

Both men and women can be game, but status for human females has rarely depended on a woman's willingness to fight.

Demure, polite, passive women are attractive to men and are generally well-liked by other women. Even today, many men will jump at the opportunity to harm a man who harms a female stranger. Because of this, many women can be assertive or make displays of gameness with relative impunity, and some become delusional about their ability to make good on their threats or defend themselves if their taunts result in violence.

Gravitas is another old word that we still use to talk about manliness, especially in actors and politicians. We say a man possesses *gravitas* when he makes us believe we should take him seriously. We get our word "gravity" from the Latin *gravitas*; it means "heavy." The Romans used *gravitas* the same way we do—to say that a man or a thing is to be taken seriously. Contrasted with the frenzied imagery of a game pit bull, it balances out our sense of what manly courage is. Courage is not only the desire to leap into battle or move up in a hierarchy; it is also about defending position. Masculine men make it clear that they are to be taken seriously, that they have weight, that they won't be pushed around. Men want other men to know that they will be "heavy" to move, and must be taken seriously.

Courage is the animating spirit of masculinity, and it is crucial to any meaningful definition of masculinity. Courage and strength are synergetic virtues. An overabundance of one is worth less without an adequate amount of the other. In any gang of men fighting for survival, courage will be esteemed and respected in the living, and it will be revered in the dead. Courage is a crucial tactical value. One can choose to be courageous, and even in its basest form, courage is a triumph over fear. It's associated with heart and spirit and passion, but it is also a drive to fight and win.

Courage is abstract, and it has many aspects, so I have summarized its definition as it relates to our attempt to understand The Way of Men and the gang ethos.

Courage is the will to risk harm in order to benefit oneself or others. In its most basic amoral form, courage is a willingness or passionate desire to fight or hold ground at any cost (gameness, heart, spirit, thumos). In its most developed, civilized and moral form courage is the considered and decisive willingness to risk harm to ensure the success or survival of a group or another person (courage, virtus, andreia).

Comparing his own experiences as a fighter to watching dogs fight, Sam Sheridan wrote:

> "They writhe furiously like snakes, twisting and spitting and slavering, growling like bears. Fury epitomized. Their tails are wagging, this is what they are meant to do, and they're fulfilling their purpose, they're *becoming*. There is blood, but the dogs don't care, turning and pinning, fighting off their backs and then clawing their way to standing [..] any pain they feel is overwhelmed by the desire to get the other dog. I know that feeling."

Plato (or Socrates) also compared men to dogs. One of the great tragedies of modernity is the lack of opportunity for men to become what they are, to do what they were bred to do, what their bodies want to do. They could be Plato's noble puppies, but they are chained to a stake in the ground—left to the madness of barking at shadows in the night, taunted by passing challenges left unresolved and whose outcomes will forever be unknown.

MASTERY

Men have always recognized themselves in animals. They have worshipped animals and claimed totemic lineage from animals. Men have traced their origins to gods who were like animals, part animal, or who could change into animals. Heracles was depicted wearing the skin of a powerful lion he killed. Norse berserkers wore the skins of wolves and bears to intimidate their enemies and inspire ferocious courage in battle. In the Aztec military, it was the elite Jaguar Warriors who went to the front. Military units and sports teams around the world adopt the names of formidable animals to represent their own gameness and strength.

Throughout this book, I have compared men to dogs and to chimpanzees. However, in sport and in war and life, there is another manly virtue that is universally and specifically human because, for the most part, it requires human intellect.

Animals succeed or fail largely due to a combination of their circumstances and their inborn genetic fitness for a given situation. An animal that is stronger, nimbler or more game will triumph over an inferior animal. We have to project our own humanity onto animals to make them masters of strategy. In all but the most intelligent animals like higher primates and orca or dolphins, what we read as skill is most often instinct—not the product of thinking or tinkering or trial and error. The desire and ability to use reason and to develop skills and technologies that allow one to gain mastery over one's circumstances—over oneself, over nature, over other men, over women— is a human virtue, although it is also man's Achilles heel.

If you ask men what it means to be good at being a man, you'll often get answers that start to sound like a set of minimum skill proficiencies in a job description.

While the job description for men undeniably changes according to time, place, and culture, the primal gang virtue that unifies them all is "being able to carry your own weight."

Women are more comfortable with accepting the benevolent aid of the group because they have always required it. A healthy adult woman must accept aid from the group if she is to carry a child, give birth, and care for an infant. And, especially when men have achieved a level of security and prosperity beyond mere survival, women have been evaluated by men based less on their utility than on more nebulous qualities like attractiveness and social charm. When they have the means, most men will happily support a woman who seems to be carefree, pretty, and charming.

This has not been the case with men. It is far rarer for women or men to volunteer to support a grown, able-bodied man. It is rarer still for them to support him without resentment. There is no point in an adult male's life when he can be excused from carrying his own weight, except when he is sick, injured, handicapped, or old. Human societies accommodate all of these exceptions, but competency has always been crucial to a man's mental health and sense of his own worth. Men want to carry their own weight, and they should be expected to. As Don Corleone might put it, women and children could afford to be careless for most of human history, but not men. Men have always had to demonstrate to the group that they could carry their own weight.

Until you can function as a competent member of the group and carry your own weight, you are a supplicant and a drag on the collective. A child is a child, but an incompetent adult is a beggar. One of the problems with massive welfare states is that they make children or beggars of us all, and as such are an affront and a barrier to adult masculinity. It has become clichéd comedy for men and women to laugh at men who are concerned with being competent. The "men refuse to stop and ask for directions" joke never seems to get old for women, who are more comfortable with dependence, or socialist types, because reducing men to a childlike state of supplication and submission to state bureaucrats is required for big-government welfare states to function. Masculine loathing of dependence is a bulwark to the therapeutic mother state.

Dependency is powerlessness. Yet, men have always been cooperative hunters, and in a survival scenario, they will fall into hierarchies based on strength and gameness. Men have a certain natural comfort with interdependency. Claims of complete independence are generally bullshit. Few of us have ever survived or would be able to survive on our own for an extended period of time. Few of us would want to. A child is completely dependent and powerless. It has no control over its own fate. Controlling one's own fate within the context of group give-and-take has to do with figuring out what you bring to the table and making yourself valuable to the group. The bare minimum required for moving from dependence to interdependence is competence and self-sufficiency—the ability to carry one's own weight.

Becoming an interdependent, rather than completely dependent, member of the group means mastering a set of useful skills and understanding some useful ideas. We send children to school to master a set of skills and a body of knowledge that we think they'll need to carry their own weight in society and function as adults. Most militaries send men to boot camp. At boot camp, men learn a basic skill set and body of knowledge necessary to function within the military. Boot camp graduates can theoretically be expected to at least carry their own weight in an offensive or defensive scenario.

Understanding The Way of Men means understanding how men evaluate each other as men, and how they accord status to men within the context of a primal history common to all men. The amoral masculine gang ethos is tactical and utilitarian. It's kind of like picking men for a sports team. Before people care about whether or not you're a good person, they want to know if you're a good player. Speculating about the morality of professional athletes is a popular form of male social gossip, but when the athletes take the field, what matters most is how they can contribute to a team's success. Men want to know if they have the physical ability, the gameness, and the mastery of the skills necessary to help the team win.

The Way of Men, the gang ethos, and the amoral tactical virtues are fundamentally about winning. Before you can have church and art and philosophy, you need to be able to survive. You need to triumph over nature and other men, or at the very least you need to be able to keep both at bay. Winning requires strength and courage, and it requires a sufficient mastery of the skills required to win.

Stated as a manly virtue:

Mastery is a man's desire and ability to cultivate and demonstrate proficiency and expertise in technics that aid in the exertion of will over himself, over nature, over women, and over other men.

Advanced levels of mastery and technics allow men to compete for improved status within the group by bringing *more* to the camp, hunt, or fight than their bodies would otherwise allow. Mastery can be supplementary—a man who can build, hunt and fight, but who can also do something else well, be it telling jokes or setting traps or making blades, is worth more to the group and is likely to have a higher status within the group than a man who can *merely* build, hunt and fight well. Mastery can also be a compensatory virtue, in the sense that a weaker or less courageous man can earn the esteem of his peers by providing something else of great value. It could well have been a runt who tamed fire or invented the crossbow or played the first music, and such a man would have earned the respect and admiration of his peers. Homer was a blind man, but his words have been valued by men for thousands of years.

Women also earn their keep through mastery of one kind or another, and mastery is by no means exclusive to men, but mastery does have a lot to do with competition for status between men. If necessity is the mother of invention, it is the need to compete for status and peer esteem—to find a valued place in the group—that drives many inventors to invent. The drive to gain control over something is part of the drive to master nature.

Strength, courage, and honor make a tidy triad, because they are all directly concerned with violence. But the picture of how men judge men as men is incomplete without some concept of mastery. Strength, gameness, and competition for status are all present in animals, but it is the conscious drive to master our world that differentiates men from beasts. Whether you're a benevolent king or a ruthless gangster, a man with a special skill, talent or technology can be as valuable as or exponentially more valuable than your toughest thug. It is mastery more often than brute strength that allows the elite to rule. Masculinity can never be separated from its connection to violence, because it is through violence that we ultimately compete for status and wield power over other men. However, mastered skills and technology provide deciding advantages in fighting, hunting, and surviving for human men.

HONOR

The idea of honor shines an ancient light so warm and golden that everyone wants to stand in it. This is the most natural desire in the world, because honor in its most inclusive sense is esteem, respect, and status. To be honored is to be respected by one's peers.

Thomas Hobbes wrote in *Leviathan* that what was honorable was, "whatsoever possession, action, or quality, is an argument and a signe of Power."[24] Hobbes believed that honor existed in a free market, where value was accorded to men based on what men had to offer and the value that other men placed on it. For Hobbes, honor was a form of deference, an acknowledgement of power and influence over other men.

In our rudimentary gang of a few men depending on each other in a hostile environment, this definition of honor is directly related to the other three masculine virtues. In a hostile environment, strength, courage, and mastery are all absolutely necessary for survival and everyone in the gang understands this to be true because external threats are regular and imminent. Men who exhibit these traits will have greater value to the group and contribute more to the group's survival and prosperity. Deference acknowledges interdependency and loyalty.

In a relatively secure society, while power ultimately comes from the ability to use violence, there are so many middlemen involved that the person who wields the most power and influence may simply be the person with the most wealth or popularity. For instance, teen singing stars and talk show hosts can wield tremendous power and influence, but their power has little or nothing to do with the esteem of the fighting men who gave the word honor its heroic glow.

According to James Bowman, there are two types of honor. *Reflexive honor* is the primitive desire to hit back when hit, to show that you will stand up for yourself.

To expand on Bowman's theory, reflexive honor is the signal of the rattlesnake, communicating a reputation for retaliation summed up by the popular old motto *Nemo me impune lacessit*, or "No one attacks me with impunity." To protect one's honor is as defensive as it is offensive—even if attack is pre-emptive, as it often is. People are more likely to leave you alone if they fear harm from you, and if men give way to you because they fear you, you will gain a certain status among men. This is equally true for a group, and in a survival scenario, it is generally a tactical advantage to appear to be fearsome. That is, it is tactically advantageous to cultivate a reputation for strength, willingness to fight, and technical mastery.

A man once said, "If I allow a man to steal my chickens, I might as well let him rape my daughters." That's reflexive honor.

Bowman also recognized the idea of *cultural honor*, which he defined as a sum of the "traditions, stories and habits of thought of a particular society about the proper and improper uses of violence."[25]

Bowman's definition of cultural honor has a moral cast to it. While

Bowman links it to violence above, he notes throughout his book that there is a conflict, especially (but not uniquely) in the Western mind between manly public honor and private, moral honor that has as much to do with one's personal philosophy and a desire to be a good person as it does with one's reputation for violent retaliation in the eyes of men. While Bowman's view of cultural honor follows from reflexive honor, cultural honor is ultimately concerned with being a good man, not being good at being a man.

Because it is linked to morality and what is valued culturally, the cultural code of honor can morph into virtually anything. We see this in the way the blood is wiped from the blade of honor today. Honor is used to indicate almost any sort of general esteem, deference, or respect. School recognition programs like The National Honor Society continue the meritocratic, hierarchical sense of honor—because study is an attempt at mastery—however gender-neutral and non-violent. The deference that Hobbes recognized in honor is now applied to abstract concepts that have little or nothing to do with traditional honor.

For instance, the slogan "Honor Diversity" is popular with gay rights advocates, who reject traditional, hierarchical ways of defining both honor and masculinity. "Honor Diversity" is an interesting slogan, because it essentially means "honor everyone and everything." If everyone is honored equally, and everyone's way of life is honored equally, honor has no hierarchy, and therefore honor has little value according to the economics of supply and demand. "Honor diversity" doesn't mean much more than "be nice."

If honor is to mean anything at all, it must be hierarchical. To be honored, as Hobbes recognized, is to be esteemed, and as humans are differently-abled and differently motivated, some will earn greater esteem than others. Americans have a strained relationship with the idea of honor. They have always been a little drunk on the idea that "all men are created equal" and politicians have spent two centuries flattering every Joe Schmoe into thinking his opinion is worth just as much as anyone else's—even when he has absolutely no idea what he is talking about. American men profess the creed of equality, but if you put a bunch of American men in a room or give them a job to do, they work out their *Lord of the Flies* hierarchies in the same way that men always have. The religion of equality gives way to the reality of meritocracy, and there's not too great a leap between Geoffroi de Charny's motto "who does more is worth more" and the rugged individualism of the American who was expected to pull himself up "by his bootstraps."

To honor a man is to acknowledge his accomplishments and recognize that he has attained a higher status within the group.

If we stop there and say that honor is merely high group status, we still have a definition of honor that would be unrecognizable to the knights, the samurai, the ancient Greeks, and the ancient Romans who—among many others—give the idea of honor the noble, mythic quality that makes it so appealing.

The reason for this is simple.

Honor has always been about the esteem of groups of men.

It probably never occurred to Hobbes to include this caveat, because, despite the occasional female monarch, he lived his entire life in a system designed to favor male interests. The thought of a system where females had an equal say has been unthinkable to all but a few before our time. Men have always ruled, and men have always determined what behaviors were honored and what behaviors were considered dishonorable. And while the specifics of these honor codes have changed as circumstances and prevailing moralities changed, the majority of men still acknowledged the fundamental tactical necessity of reflexive honor. They still judged each other as men according to the basic masculine virtues of strength, courage and mastery.

When the word "honor" is connected to the word "culture" and framed as a negative, social scientists seem to be more comfortable with a definition of honor similar to the one I'm presenting here. Recently, an article linking a higher rate of accidental death in males to risk-taking and honor culture in southern states[26] received attention from mainstream news outlets.[27] The researchers in question defined this honor culture according to a cultural emphasis on "the relentless, and sometimes violent, defense of masculine reputation, which is presumably a social adaptation to an environment characterized by scarce resources, frequent intergroup aggression (e.g., raiding), and the absence of the rule of law."[28] They hypothesized that men from honor cultures would be more likely to engage in risky behaviors because "risky behaviors provide social proof of strength and fearlessness." While the study revealed the biases of its authors by focusing on the white honor culture of Southern Ulster-Scots and avoiding any discussion of honor cultures among Latino prison gangs, African warlords or Islamic terrorists, the researchers seemed to agree that honor among men tends to be defined by a concern with maintaining a reputation for strength and courage (two of our other three masculine virtues).

Bowman and others have written that "honor depends on the honor group."[29] The honor group is the male gang, and honor cultures are about status within a given gang of men. What the sociologists were essentially saying in their study of "honor states" is that some men care more about what other men think of them—specifically, their reputation for strength, honor and mastery—than others. Honor groups depend on a sense of shared identity. In a cosmopolitan scenario where frequent travel, fleeting connections, and temporary alliances are the norm, the *us* vs. *them* never quite takes shape on the direct interpersonal level. Instead, the honor group is ritualized or metaphorical—as with sports teams and political parties and ideological positions. These allegiances can be abandoned easily, and personal accountability is minimal. Honor relies on face-to-face connections and the possibility of shame or dishonor in the eyes of other men. This partially explains why men who have grown up together in the same ghetto block or the same rural area, or who have spent time bunked together, will be more likely to be concerned with honor than more mobile men who travel a lot, or men who only spend time with other men in the presence of females.

As it relates to understanding the masculine ethos:

Honor is a man's reputation for strength, courage, and mastery within the context of an honor group comprised primarily of other men.

Stated as a masculine virtue:

Honor is a concern for one's reputation for strength, courage, and mastery within the context of an honor group comprised primarily of other men.

There are moral codes and cultural codes of honor that factor into men's estimation of the men within their honor groups, but the point here is to reduce masculinity to first principles without getting lost in a morass of variable cultural honor codes. What is common to the honor of the Mafioso and the honor of the knight, to the honor of American founding father Alexander Hamilton[30] and the honor of any naked savage is a concern for one's reputation as a man of strength, courage, and mastery, and how it relates to a man's sense of worthiness and belonging within the context of a male honor group.

Understanding Dishonor

Part of the reason that honor is a virtue rather than merely a state of affairs is that showing concern for the respect of your peers is a show of loyalty and an indication of belonging—of being *us* rather than *them*. It is a show of deference. Hobbes noted that men honored each other by seeking each other's counsel and by imitating each other. Caring about what the men around you think of you is a show of respect, and conversely, not caring what other men think of you is a sign of disrespect.

In a survival band, it is tactically advantageous to maintain a reputation for being strong, courageous, and masterful as a group. A man who does not care for his own reputation makes his team look weak by association. Dishonor and disregard for honor are dangerous for a survival band or a fighting team because the appearance of weakness invites attack. At the personal, intragroup level, the appearance of weakness or submissiveness invites other men to assert their interests over your own.

The tactical problems presented by the appearance of weakness as a group explain, to some extent, the visceral response many men have to displays of flamboyant effeminacy. The word effeminacy is a bit misleading here, because this really isn't about women. The dislike of what is commonly called effeminacy is about male status anxiety and practical concerns about tactical vulnerabilities, and it is more accurate to discuss dishonor in terms of *deficient masculinity* and *flamboyant dishonor*.

Deficient masculinity is simply a lack of strength, courage, or mastery.

Because masculinity and honor are by nature hierarchical, all men are in some way deficient in masculinity compared to a higher status man. There is always a higher status man, if not in your group, then in another, and if not in this way then in that way, and if not now, then eventually. No one is the strongest, most courageous, *and* the smartest or most masterful man—though some men are closer to the ideal or perfect "form" of masculinity than others. Masculinity in the perfect ideal is aspirational, not attainable. The point is to be better, stronger, more courageous, more masterful—to achieve greater honor.

The men who possess the least of these qualities or suffer from an excessive lack of one in particular are the men who other men don't want to be. They are furthest from the ideal. So long as they don't openly despise the ideal or attempt to move the goalposts to appear "more masculine" by creating some new artificial standard, men will tend to include and help members of their gang or tribe who are unusually deficient in strength, courage or mastery. The lowest status men within a group are still usually included in the group unless they bring shame to the group as a whole—thus endangering the group, at least in theory—or fail so miserably that they become an excessive burden. Most high-status men are not monsters, and most low-status men don't want to be a burden on others (because dependency is slavery), so men who are not good at being men generally try to find some way to make themselves useful or at least tolerable to a given group of men. Think of the funny fat guys and the frail artists and the nurturing fellows who make sure everything is in order for the men of action. All large groups of men seem to have members who assume these kinds of low-status roles while remaining part of the honor group.

Deficient masculinity is undesirable and results in low status. Men despise deficient masculinity in themselves because they would naturally rather be stronger, more courageous, and more masterful. Deficient masculinity rarely arouses hate or anger within a male group, though it may result in some general frustration.

Flamboyant Dishonor

Deficient masculinity is trying and failing. Failure is part of trying, and while men tease and goad each other, no man who has become masterful at anything has achieved that mastery without a certain amount of failure along the way.

Male groups are hierarchical, so while greater dominance is desirable, a certain amount of submission is essential to any co-operative group of men. Unless some men give way to others, you'll end up with too many chiefs and not enough Indians. Honor as a virtue means caring about what other men think of you, trying to earn their esteem, and asserting yourself as best you can to achieve the highest relative position within the group.

Flamboyant dishonor is not a failure of strength or courage. Men who are flamboyantly dishonorable are flagrant in their disregard for the esteem of their male peers. What we often call effeminacy is a theatrical rejection of the masculine hierarchy and manly virtues. Masculinity is religious, and flamboyantly dishonorable men are blasphemers. Flamboyant dishonor is an insult to the core values of the male group.

Flamboyant dishonor is an openly expressed lack of concern for one's reputation for strength, courage, and mastery within the context of an honor group comprised primarily of other men.

In 1994, Michael Kimmel wrote an essay which provocatively asserted that "homophobia is a central organizing principle of our cultural definition of manhood." He went on to clarify that this homophobia had little or nothing to do with homosexual acts or an actual fear of homosexuals. He wrote, "Homophobia is the fear that other men will unmask us, emasculate us, reveal to the world that we do not measure up, that we are not real men. We are afraid to let other men see that fear."[31]

Why call it homophobia?

The kind of masculine status anxiety Kimmel wrote about has much to do with the way men fumble to translate the honor of the small, bonded male gang into a complex modern society full of mixed messages and overlapping male groups. This fear is a fear of the unknown. In an established, tightly bonded male group, men know about where they stand in the hierarchy. There's nowhere to hide, so there is less fear of being revealed as a fraud, and like some kind of primal sports ranking system, men are constantly tested against one another and against external forces.

I've observed this in the few brief introductions I've had to Brazilian *jiu-jitsu*, in gyms where everyone rolls with everyone. Men find out quickly who is good, and who isn't. There is no hiding or pretending, and it doesn't matter whether or not your Internet profile picture looks tough or if you put on a good show— because here is this guy who is choking you out. You are revealed as what you are, and all that remains is to improve. The only way you can increase your status within the group is to try harder and get better.

Flamboyant dishonor is a little bit like walking into that room full of men who are trying to get better at *jiu-jitsu* and insisting that they stop what they are doing and pay attention to your fantastic new tap-dancing routine. The flamboyantly dishonorable man seeks attention for something the male group doesn't value, or which isn't appropriate at a given time.

At the primal level, flamboyant dishonor presents tactical problems for the group. By outwardly and theatrically rejecting the core masculine values, particularly strength and courage, the flamboyantly dishonorable male advertises weakness and a propensity for submission to outside watchers. Any honest student of human (and in many cases, primate) body language will be forced to recognize that the postures, gestures and intonations of males generally regarded as effeminate are, in fact, postures, gestures, and intonations that communicate submissiveness. Humans are complicated, and when push comes to shove, stereotypically effeminate males are not always as submissive as their body language would seem to indicate. However, submissiveness is what they advertise.

This submissiveness correlates with male homosexuality, and the problems men have with male homosexuality—aside from concerns about unsolicited advances—are mostly related to the perception of an over-willingness to submit to other men. There are extremely submissive or flamboyantly dishonorable effeminate heterosexual men. Kimmel, for instance, is heterosexual but flamboyantly dishonorable. His wrists are limp, his gestures are airy, his demeanor is precious, and he has devoted his entire career to the open rejection of the manly virtues and a persistent devaluing of male honor codes. I do not need to insult him. None of these qualities are negative according to his own views, and I am certain he is proud of his life's work. He is a perfect example of a heterosexual male who flagrantly rejects the gang virtues of strength, courage, mastery, and honor.

The man who flamboyantly rejects the honor codes of the group can obviously not be trusted to "snap to" in a state of emergency. Dishonor is disloyalty. A man who not only openly refuses to strive to be as strong, courageous, and competent as he can, but who flaunts these codes theatrically for all to see is a weak link. He makes his peers seem more vulnerable for tolerating vulnerability, and more cowardly for tolerating cowardice. He brings shame on the group, and with shame comes danger, because public displays of weakness and cowardice invite attack.

This tactical reasoning goes a long way toward explaining why men who function successfully within male honor groups make a big show of rejecting and distancing themselves from males who are flamboyantly dishonorable. By expelling effeminate males from the gang or by shaming them and pushing them to the fringes of a particular group, the group projects strength and unity. The group demonstrates that "we do not tolerate unmanly men here."

The shunning of homosexuals and perceived homosexuals is generally justified with appeals to divine or natural laws. That's spin that absolves men of responsibility for social cruelty to members of their own tribe. When men reject effeminate men, they are rejecting weakness, casting it out, and cleansing themselves of its corrosive stigma.

In many societies that have openly tolerated effeminacy, flamboyantly effeminate males have been relegated to a half-man, half-woman status and given a special role. The Native American *berdake*, for example, were regarded as neither man nor woman. They were usually men; they dressed differently to distinguish themselves from men, they generally did what was considered woman's work within the village, and they were often regarded as serving a "mediating role between men and woman."[32] Indian *hijras* are another example of flamboyantly dishonorable (or gender non-conforming, if you prefer the feminist lingo) males who are accepted in society so long as they accept a special gender status and exist apart from normal men.

Honor is a powerful concept because it is connected to every man's primal need to demonstrate that he is of value to the group—that he is more of an asset than a liability. Women have a separate value to men, and that has nothing to do with their ability to demonstrate strength, courage, or mastery. Men who are deficient or handicapped in some way can deliver value in other ways. Most men care about being seen by other men as being strong, courageous and competent because these tactical virtues have been essential to their role as men and their very survival for most of human history. In a war or in an emergency, these virtues would still be of primary importance, and all other virtues would be comparatively incidental.

In less dire times, as opportunities for men to demonstrate the tactical virtues decrease, honor broadens its scope. Men still struggle to show other men that they are worthy. They still struggle to show that they are worth having around, worthy of belonging to the group—a valued member of "us." When there is less hunting and fighting to do, men attempt to increase their value to other men by showing that they are good people or good citizens—good members of the tribe. They try to show that they are good men. Earning and keeping a reputation as a good man overlaps conceptually with honor because it is another way to add value and show worth to other men. Honor as a virtue is a demonstration of group loyalty, so it naturally expands to include other demonstrations of loyalty to the values of the group—from piously praising the tribal gods to "standing up for what is right" according to the group's ethical codes.

Still, honor at its root is about showing men that you are good at being a man and good at filling man's first role on the perimeter. Showing other men that you are a good man is an outgrowth of that. Being a good man is related to honor, but it is not the root of honor. We care what other men think of us, first and foremost, because men have always depended on each other to survive. It is triumph over nature and triumph over other men—it is survival and prosperity and life itself—that give honor the golden glow which draws men to it and repels them from dishonor.

"We see men of all kinds of professed creeds attain to almost all degrees of worth or worthlessness under any of them. This is not what I call religion, this profession and assertion; which is often only a profession and assertion from the outworks of the man, from the mere argumentative region of him, if even so deep as that. But the thing a man does practically believe (and this is often enough without asserting it even to himself, much less to others); the thing a man does practically lay to heart, and know for certain, concerning his vital relations to this mysterious Universe, and his duty and destiny there, that is in all cases the primary thing for him, and creatively determines all the rest. That is his religion; or, it may be, his mere skepticism and no-religion: the manner it is in which he feels himself to be spiritually related to the Unseen World or No-World; and I say, if you tell me what that is, you tell me to a very great extent what the man is, what the kind of things he will do is."

—Thomas Carlyle, *On Heroes, Hero-Worship and the Heroic in History.*

ON BEING A GOOD MAN

Reducing masculinity to a handful of tactical virtues may seem crude, thuggish, and uncivilized. What about moral virtue? What about justice, humility, charity, faith, righteousness, honesty, and temperance?

Aren't these manly virtues, too?

Men aren't heartless monsters, and they aren't machines. Men think about more than hunting and killing and defending. Men are capable of compassion as well as cruelty.

Thinking men ask "why." It's not always enough to win. Men want to believe that they are *right*—and that their enemies are *wrong*. To separate *us* from *them*, men find moral fault in their enemies and create codes of conduct to distinguish themselves as good men. One of the finest examples of this is the Christian knight—an ascetic committed to piety and violence, fighting in shining armor for goodness with God on his side. Most men would agree that it is better to be a good man who stands up to bad men. They would rather be heroes than villains. Most men want to see themselves as good men fighting for something greater than survival or gain.

When you ask men about what makes a *real* man, a lot of them will get up on their high horses and start talking about what it means to be a good man.

"A real man would never hit a woman."

"A man who doesn't spend time with his family can never be a real man."

"A real man takes responsibility for his actions."

"A real man pays his debts."

"Real men love Jesus."

However, if you ask the same men to list their favorite "guy movies," many of them will include films like *The Godfather, Scarface, Goodfellas,* and *Fight Club.*

Don Corleone, Tommy DeVito, and Henry Hill were all ruthless racketeers. Scarface was a murdering drug lord. Tyler Durden was basically a domestic terrorist. There are scores of popular gang and heist flicks, among them: *Oceans 11* (and *12,* and *13*), *Snatch, Smoking Aces, The Italian Job, Heat, Ronin, The Sting, The Usual Suspects, Reservoir Dogs* and *Pulp Fiction.*[33] The calculating, morally ambiguous hitman for hire has found an especially sympathetic place in the cinematic pantheon of manliness: *The Professional, The Matador, In Bruges, The Mechanic, The American, Collateral, Road to Perdition, No Country for Old Men.* Hitman was both a film and a video game. Two of the best-selling video game franchises during the last decade were *Assassin's Creed* and *Grand Theft Auto. Sons of Anarchy,* a show about a motorcycle gang, was popular on television. Are its characters unmanly because they are outlaws? What about Tony from *The Sopranos* or Al Swearengen from *Deadwood?*

Was Darth Vader a pussy?

Despite the moral posturing, men are attracted to these characters precisely because they are manly. Bad guys tend to operate in brutal, indelicate, and unmoderated boys' clubs, and they seem to be particularly concerned with the business of being a man. Gangsters are status-conscious, aggressive, tactically-oriented, ballsy, brother-bonded men's men. The loner hitmen are portrayed as capable but careful smooth operators who are masters of their dangerous craft. They are not good men, but they are good at doing the kinds of things that have been demanded of men throughout human history. They are not good men, but they are good at being men.

Before film, men and boys were thrilled by tales of outlaws, pirates, highwaymen, and thieves. Whether these stories were romanticized or spun as cautionary tales, they captured the male imagination with adventurous accounts of daring and mischievous virility.

In Shakespeare's *The Life of Henry the Fifth*, the King promised his enemies that unless they surrendered, his men would rape their shrieking daughters, dash the heads of their old men, and impale their naked babies on pikes. Today, if a military leader made a promise so indelicate, he would be fired and publicly denounced as an evil, broken psychopath. I can't call Henry an unmanly character with a straight face.

Consider also the case of the prisoner. Do you truly believe that men who negotiate a violent, all-male world every day are less manly than a nice guy who works 9 to 5 in a cubicle farm and spends his free time doing whatever his wife tells him to do?

What about suicide bombers? I'd say that hijacking a plane with a box knife and flying it into a building takes *balls of steel*. I don't have to like it, but if I'm being honest with myself, I can't call those guys unmanly. Enemies of my tribe, yes. Unmanly, no. Remember that there are hundreds of thousands of men and boys who regard suicide bombers as brave, martyred heroes who took substantial risks and made the ultimate sacrifice for a cause. We think of them as evil and flatter ourselves by calling them *cowardly* because they aren't on our team, because they don't share all of our values, and because they endanger our collective interests.

We want our external enemies to be defective and unsympathetic. Many have written about our tendency to dehumanize our foes. Emasculating them is another aspect of that—it adds insult to injury. We also want to puff ourselves up and psych them out. It's a good strategy. Insulting a man's honor—his masculine identity—is a good way to test him. It's a good way to get his blood up. It's a good way to pick a fight.

We want our villains within to be equally unsympathetic. Portraying bad men as unmanly men is a good way to dissuade young men from behaving badly. Making your own cultural heroes seem bigger than life men elevates group pride and morale. It makes sense to want your young men to emulate men who champion your people's values, and young men especially tend to choose the stronger horse.

Cultures have wrestled with the idea of what it means to be a good man for thousands of years. Waller R. Newell, a professor of political science and philosophy, collected a broad range of thinking on the topic for his book *What is a Man? 3,000 Years of Wisdom on the Art of Manly Virtue*. Newell criticized those who came of age in the 1960s for establishing a cultural orthodoxy prone to believing that "nothing just, good, or true" had happened before their time, and for causing the "disappearance of the positive tradition of manliness through relentless simplification and caricature."[34] He showed what he referred to as an "unbroken pedigree in the Western conception of what it means to be a man," which he defined as "honor tempered by prudence, ambition tempered by compassion for the suffering and the oppressed, love restrained by delicacy and honor toward the beloved."[35] His sourcebook was filled with selections from Plato, Aristotle, Marcus Aurelius, Francis Bacon, Geoffrey Chaucer, William Shakespeare, Benjamin Franklin, Ralph Waldo Emerson, Winston Churchill, John F. Kennedy, and many others.

There is a movement to reclaim this idea of virtuous manhood—to show young men how to be good and manly men. In 2009, venture capitalist Tom Matlack started a "four-pronged effort to foster a discussion about manhood," called The Good Men Project. The Good Men Project currently exists as a foundation, an online magazine, a documentary film, and a book. The book is filled with stories of men who are struggling to be good men in the 21st Century, and trying to figure out what that means.

The Art of Manliness website was founded by Brett McKay and his wife Kate in 2008, and boasts some 90,000 subscribers.[36] The McKays have published two books offering their take on the subject of manliness: *The Art of Manliness – Classic Skills and Manners for the Modern Man*, and *The Art of Manliness - Manvotionals: Timeless Wisdom and Advice on Living the 7 Manly Virtues*. The site itself reveres good, manly historical figures like "Rough Rider" Theodore Roosevelt, and it has a nostalgic feel to it. It's a bit like a Boy Scout handbook for adult males, offering advice and "how to" articles to help out men who are trying to be good protectors, providers, husbands, and fathers. An Art of Manliness workout isn't just a workout; it becomes "hero training."

I asked Brett McKay about what he thought the difference was between being a good man and being good at being a man. He said that being good at being a man means, "being proficient in your ability to earn and keep your culture's idea of manhood." He elaborated, noting that while there were cross-cultural similarities, "Being good at being a man for the Kalahari bushman means being able to be persistent and hunt successfully. Being good at being a man for a man living in suburban Ohio probably means holding a job down to support a family, being able to fix things around the house, or if he's single, being adept at interacting with women." McKay told me he thought being a good man was simpler.

He wrote: "developing virtues like honesty, resilience, courage, compassion, discipline, justice, temperance, etc. A man can be a very virtuous and upright man, but be horrible at "being good at being a man." Maybe he can't hunt or he's terrible around women or can't use a hammer to save his life. It's also possible to have a man who's good at being a man, but isn't a good man. You can be the best hunter or mechanic in the world, but if you lie, cheat, steal, you're not a good man."[37]

McKay seemed to say that being good at being a man is like fulfilling a job description, defined by what your culture needs (or wants) men to do, and being a good man has more to do with the kind of moral virtues that Newell advocated. A man can fail at the job of being a man, but still be a good person. I use person here, because these moral values are fairly gender neutral. Perhaps, along these lines of thinking, being a good man is a matter of balancing the cultural demands of manhood with a private commitment to moral uprightness.

McKay's positive prescription for manliness is a welcome change from mainstream "men's magazines," which are more interested in creating sociopathic metrosexual super-consumers than writing positively about manhood. I'd agree with McKay that being good at being a man is rather like a job description, and that the description changes a great deal from culture to culture.

However, stopping there plays into the hands of those who say that being a man can mean anything anyone wants it to mean. Is manliness so flexible a concept that a community can rewrite the job description however they wish? Not if we accept any model of human nature that acknowledges differences between male and female psychology. Over the past few decades, Americans have transitioned to a service economy, and educators treated boys like naughty girls with attitude problems. Males have become less interested in educational achievement, less engaged in political life, less concerned about careers, and more interested in forms of entertainment that feature vicarious gang drama—like video games and spectator sports.[38]

Further, if the "job description" of being a man is written in such a way that the qualities which make a good man are basically identical to the qualities that make a good woman, then those qualities are more about being a good person than anything else. It is good to be honest, just, and kind, but these virtues don't have much specifically to do with being a man. Manliness can't merely be synonymous with "good behavior."

I was raised by a decent family in rural Pennsylvania. I went to Sunday school. I was taught to be polite and respectful to others. I over-tip even when I get crappy service in restaurants, I hold doors for little old ladies, and I'm honest to a fault. When I treat people poorly, I feel bad about it—unless they really had it coming. Like many men, I rebelled against my parent's values when I was younger. However, perhaps like Brett McKay or Tom Matlack, when I later began thinking seriously about masculinity and what it meant, the following phrase kept popping into my head: "I can't think of anything better to be than a good man."

I still can't. My first attempts to describe the value of traditional masculinity in print were laced with the kind of homespun morality I grew up with.

I respect men who try their damnedest to be good men—even when I don't agree with them concerning every little detail about what that means. A lot of men choose careers in law enforcement, firefighting, teaching, or even the military because they truly want to be good men. Wars, laws, and policies aren't always just, but I have to tip my hat to the men who rescue civilians and pull kids out of burning buildings. Only broken hysterics refer to all soldiers and cops as "cannon fodder" or "pigs" or "tools."

However, unless self-sacrifice and restraint are to be masculinity's defining qualities—unless masculinity is to be an ascetic discipline and nothing more—there is a point somewhere down a road of diminishing returns that being a good man is no longer a good trade. There's a point where a man who wants to "feel useful" ends up "feeling used." When the system no longer offers men what they want, how long can you expect them to perform tricks for a pat on the head? How long until the neglected, starving dog turns on its master?

I agree with Newell that there is a long, proud tradition of moral masculinity in the West, and from what I can gather, there are comparable traditions in the East. Muslim men pray five times a day because they, too, want to be good men in their own way.

However, Newell's pitch itself contains a built-in duality: honor *tempered* by prudence, ambition *tempered* by compassion for the suffering and the oppressed, love *restrained* by delicacy—and so forth. Civilized religious and secular attempts to show men how to be good men all seem to include these kinds of checks and balances. These "good man" codes tell men to be manly—but not *too manly*. They advocate restraint. Restraint of what? It seems as though in one hand we have morality, and in the other we have something else—a kind of maleness that must be guarded against.

If we allow the moralizers of masculinity to define masculinity for us, we either give ourselves over to the "one true code of masculinity" and become completely ethnocentric about it—which would be the historical norm—or we end up with an endless number of "masculinities," get bogged down in the details of their myriad contradictions and declare, as one famous transgendered sociologist has, "that masculinity is not a coherent object about which a generalizing science can be produced."[39] It is true that if a word or concept can mean anything, it means nothing. Raewyn "Bob" Connell wrote that, "claims about a universal basis of masculinity tell us more about the ethos of the claimant than anything else."[40] Connell was a feminist pacifist who advocated the de-gendering of society, as well as a man who wanted to be a woman. He eventually de-gendered himself. His claims about the non-existence of a universal basis of masculinity also revealed his own ethos.

All men and women have emotional and material interests when it comes to how masculinity is constructed or deconstructed. True objectivity on this subject is a more or less successful pose. We all have a horse in the race.

For whatever it is worth, scientific evidence for biological *differences* between the sexes and cross-cultural *commonalities* between men has continued to build since Connell published *Masculinities* in 1995, and it is not difficult to find repeated themes in the "hegemonic masculinities" of cultures across the world and throughout history. It is far more difficult to find "masculinities" that have nothing in common. Technologies and customs vary, but the similarities between cultural ideas of manhood offer more in the way of explaining what it means to be good at being a man than the ephemeral differences. What they have in common has more to do with the gang—with hunting and fighting, with drawing and defending the boundary between us and them—than it has to do with any culturally specific moral or ethical system.

It's dishonest to pretend that men who don't meet a given set of moral standards are unmanly men. Men may say that immoral men are not real men, but their behavior—including the public admiration for the virility of roguish and criminal types—shows that they don't quite believe this.

To truly understand The Way of Men, we must look for where the masculinity of the gangster overlaps with the masculinity of the chivalrous knight, where modern ideas overlap with ancient ones. We must look at the phenomenon of masculinity *amorally* and as dispassionately as we can. We must find what Man knows for certain, concerning his vital relations to this mysterious Universe. The "religion" of Man is not a moral code, though a man may follow his own code to his death. A man struggles to maintain his honor—his reputation as a man—because some part of him is struggling to earn and maintain a position of value, his status and his sense of belonging within the primal gang. Men want to be good men because good men are well regarded, but being a good man isn't the same as being good at being a man.

There is a difference between being a good man and being good at being a man.[41]

Being a good man has to do with ideas about morality, ethics, religion, and behaving productively within a given civilizational structure. Being a good man may or may not have anything at all to do with the natural role of men in a survival scenario. It is possible to be a good man without being particularly good at being a man. This is an area where men who were good at being men have sought counsel from priests, philosophers, shamans, writers, and historians. The productive synergy between these kinds of men is sadly lost when men of words and ideas pit themselves against men of action, or vice versa. Men of ideas and men of action have much to learn from each other, and the truly great are men of both action and abstraction.

Being good at being a man is about being willing and able to fulfill the natural role of men in a survival scenario. Being good at being a man is about showing other men that you are the kind of guy they'd want on their team if the shit hits the fan. Being good at being a man isn't a quest for moral perfection, it's about fighting to survive. Good men admire or respect bad men when they demonstrate strength, courage, mastery or a commitment to the men of their own renegade tribes. A concern with being good at being a man is what good guys and bad guys have in common.

* * *

Given enough time, every gang will create some sort of moral code or system of rules to govern its members. Men want to believe they are in the right, and they distinguish themselves by cobbling together some idea of what it means to be right.

In early *mafia* culture, honor meant loyalty "more important than blood ties." Mobsters swore not to make money from prostitution or sleep with each other's wives.[42] They were expected to be family men and were discouraged from womanizing. If the quote "A man who doesn't spend time with his family can never be a real man," seemed familiar, that's because it was from *The Godfather*.

Yakuza gangs modeled themselves after samurai, and increased their social standing within the larger community by showing generosity and compassion toward the weak and disadvantaged.[43]

One Mexican gang, known as *La Familia Michoacana*, recently preached "family values," passed out their own version of the Bible, and used some of their profits to help the poor. [44]The leaders of *La Familia* are known to have been influenced by the "macho Christian writing of contemporary American author John Eldredge."[45]

In dire times, men who are not good at being men won't last long enough to worry about being good men. Strength makes all other values possible. As Han said in *Enter the Dragon*: "Who knows what delicate wonders have died out of the world, for want of the strength to survive?"

Men who have accomplished the first job of being men—men who have made survival possible—can and do often concern themselves with being good men. As the bloody boundary between threat and safety moves outward, men have the time and the luxury to cultivate civilized, "higher" virtues.

Gangs of men with separate identities and interests of their own are always a threat to established interests. To protect the interests of those who run our civilized, highly regulated world, men and women are mixed to discourage gang formation. Feminists, pacifists, and members of the privileged classes recognize that brother-bonded men who are good at being men will always be a threat, but forget that some of those men are necessary to create and maintain order in the first place. There is a call to do away with what even the United Nations has deemed "outmoded stereotypes" of masculinity that are associated with violence.[46] "Outmoded" is a word you'll see frequently in academic writing about masculinity. So-called experts talk about manhood like it was last year's fad, in part because they subscribe to convenient but discredited blank slate theories about gender being "as lightly linked to sex as are the clothing, the manners, and the form of head-dress that a society at a given period assigns to either sex."[47]

Both men and women have attempted to refashion men to suit their dream of a perfect world. No matter what creed they profess, whether they want to make "Democratic Men" or "Fierce Gentlemen" or "Inner Warriors" they can't seem to escape the gravitational pull of some basic ideas about the underlying *religion* of men.[48] To appeal to men, they speak of strength and courage. The moralizers and reimaginers of masculinity play on a man's primal concern with his status within the male group, concern for his reputation, his distaste for being seen as weak, fearful, or inept—they appeal to his sense of *honor*. Their moralized and reimagined interpretations of strength and courage are simply tamed and pacified versions of the old gang virtues, suited to civilized life in a time of peace, plenty, and the sharing of political and economic power with women.

To protect and serve their own interests, the wealthy and privileged have used feminists and pacifists to promote a masculinity that has nothing to do with being good at being a man, and everything to do with being what they consider a "good man." Their version of a good man is isolated from his peers, emotional, effectively impotent, easy to manage, and tactically inept.

A man who is more concerned with being a good man than being good at being a man makes a very well-behaved slave.

There has always been a push and pull between civilized virtues and tactical gang virtues. However, the kind of masculinity acceptable to civilized societies is in many cases related to survival band masculinity. Civilized masculinity requires male gang dramas to become increasingly controlled, vicarious, and metaphorical. Human societies start with the gang, and then grow into nations with sports and a climate of political, artistic, and ideological competition. Eventually—as we see today— average men end up with economic competition and a handful of masturbatory outlets for their caged manhood. When a civilization fails, gangs of young men are there to scavenge its ruins, mark new perimeters, and restart the world.

"Remove justice, and what are kingdoms but gangs of criminals on a large scale? What are criminal gangs but petty kingdoms? A gang is a group of men under command of a leader, bound by a compact of association, in which the plunder is divided according to an agreed convention.

If this villainy wins so many recruits from the ranks of the demoralized that it acquires territory, establishes a base, captures cities and subdues people, it then openly arrogates itself the title of kingdom, which is conferred on it in the eyes of the world, not by the renouncing of aggression but by the attainment of impunity"

—St. Augustine, *City of God*. 4-4.

THUG LIFE : THE STORY OF ROME

AS THE STORY GOES, Rome was founded by a gang.

The Romans believed that Romulus and Remus were the distant descendants of Aeneas, who wandered the Mediterranean with a small band of survivors after the ruin of Troy. These exiled Trojans—the few remaining ambassadors of a proud but defeated tradition—were guided by the gods to Latium, where they intermingled with the Latin people of Italy. The former Trojans thrived there—and founded the settlement of Alba Longa—just southeast of modern Rome.

Many generations passed, and the eldest son of each king took the throne until Amulius ousted his older brother Numitor. Amulius murdered Numitor's sons and forced his daughter Rhea Silvia to become a Vestal Virgin, assuring that the exiled Numitor would have no heirs to challenge his own. However, Rhea gave birth to twin boys, and rather than admit an indiscretion, she claimed that they were fathered by Mars, the god of war. King Amulius didn't buy her story. He had her chained and ordered her sons to be drowned in the Tiber river. The men charged with this task left the boys exposed in the swampy shallows of the flooded river and assumed the current would carry them to their deaths. According to legend, it was there that they were rescued by a thirsty she-wolf and suckled on her hairy dugs. The grandsons of Numitor were then discovered by shepherds who took the boys in and raised them as their own.

Thanks in part to a vigorous country life, Romulus and Remus grew into strong young men known for hunting and for fearlessly confronting "wild beasts." They also gained a reputation for attacking robbers, taking their loot, and sharing it with all of their shepherd pals. The generous twins were also fun to be around, and their merry band grew.

During a festival, they were ambushed by the bitter robbers ,and Remus was brought before King Amulius on poaching charges. While Remus was in custody, Numitor suspected who the twins really were.

Meanwhile, Romulus organized his band of shepherds to kill Amulius and free his brother. The shepherds entered the city separately and gathered together at the last moment to overwhelm Amulius' guard. Romulus succeeded in killing the tyrant king, and after learning his true heritage, he restored the kingship to his grandfather Numitor.

The reunited twins then decided to found a city together on the land where they were raised. However, the two men quarreled over its naming, and the dispute became heated. The brothers challenged each other, and in the end, Romulus triumphed, killing his beloved twin brother.

Romulus and his friends then set to work organizing the government of the new city that bore his name.

According to the historian Livy, one of the first things that Romulus did after making some rudimentary fortifications was to establish the religious rites that would be celebrated by the people of Rome. In addition to the rites honoring the local gods, Romulus chose to observe the Greek rites of the heroic god-man Hercules, known for his great strength and for his "virtuous deeds."[49]

After identifying a constellation of gods and setting a rough spiritual course for his tribe, Romulus advertised the city of Rome as an asylum where all men, freeborn or slave, could start a new life. A motley collection of immigrants from neighboring tribes travelled to Rome, and he selected the best men to help him rule. These men were made *senators* and designated "fathers" (*patres*) of the Roman tribe. Their heirs would be known as patricians. With the city fathers, he created order through law.

Lacking women, the men of Rome knew their city would die with them. Romulus sent out envoys to surrounding communities to secure wives for his men. Their offers of marriage were refused, however, because the young men of Rome had no prospects, no reputations, and were generally regarded as a dangerous band of low-born men. Insulted, Romulus and his men hatched a scheme, and invited the people of neighboring communities to a festival. During the festival, they seized the unmarried girls. Their parents were furious, and the other tribes affected made war with Rome, but Rome prevailed over all militarily except the Sabines, with whom the women themselves helped to make peace to save both their fathers and their new husbands. The Sabines decided to join the Romans, and it was through this successful "rape" of the Sabine women that Romulus ensured the future of his new tribe.

Romulus continued to strengthen and defend his tribe through calculated military action, and he was loved by the rank and file of his men-at-arms. These rough men—Romulus's big gang— secured the city and made its growth possible. They were Rome's guardian class, and their unbeatable fighting spirit would characterize the Roman people for centuries.

One day, as he prepared to review his troops, Romulus disappeared with a violent clap of thunder. Livy suspected that he was torn apart at the hands of his senators, who were contentious and tended to conspire, as men close to power often do. The Roman people preferred to remember Romulus as a great man of divine lineage who lived among the people as one of them, who was known for his meritorious works and courage in battle, and who finally took his rightful place among the gods.

There are many founding myths of cities, and countless myths that establish a totemic lineage of a particular people. In the absence of certain recorded history, this is the myth that Romans chose to believe about themselves. It is the spirit of the tale that endures, and it can tell us something about The Way of Men.

Romulus and Remus were betrayed and abandoned. They were left to die and saved by a wolf. Livy admits that the wolf might have easily been a country whore, but it doesn't really matter—they were raised wild. Romulus and Remus were raised "country." They had practical know-how, and they knew the value of a hard day's work. They were given a simple upbringing, uncomplicated by court politics or the soft moral equivocation that attends urban commerce. They were virile and upright youth.

The early life of Romulus and Remus is a Robin Hood story. They roughed up other men, seized their stolen loot, and shared it with their poor friends. They were alpha males, natural leaders of men. They were tough, but they weren't bullies. They were the kind of men who other men look up to and want to be around. They were the kind of guys who men choose to lead of their own free will. They had heroic qualities, but they were as flawed as any men—and when the brothers fought for status, as brothers often do, one of them had to lose.

Romulus' "merry men" were basically a gang. They were a rowdy bunch of country boys who came out of nowhere to attack a king and upset the *status quo*. When Romulus staked out his territory and announced that it would be an asylum, he attracted hooligans with little money or status of their own. Some were former slaves. Some could have been wanted men. They had little to lose, everything to gain, and no real investment in the communities they came from. Rome was Deadwood; it was The Wild West. Romulus organized these unruly men and established a hierarchy. He founded a culture, a religion, a group identity.

Like any bunch of young men, Romulus' thugs had reproductive interests. Romulus tried the nice route, sending ambassadors out to inquire about getting his men some wives, but his men were laughed out of town. No father of means was going to send his daughter out to some camp to marry a man with no prospects. So Romulus took the women. The Romans were able to keep the women and start families because they were strong and effective fighters. They didn't give in. They fought for a new future, and they won.

The Roman tribe used violence and cunning to expand its borders, and men from many tribes became Romans. The expansion of Rome served the interests of the descendants of the tribal fathers: the patrician class. However, Roman economic and military power also benefitted many other citizens and non-citizens living within Roman territory. Protected by Roman might, men were able to specialize and live their lives as laborers, craftsmen, farmer, and traders. Many men were able to live relatively non-violent lives. The Roman definition of manliness expanded to include ethical virtues that were less specifically male, but more harmonious with a more complex civilization.

However, the Romans who rested in the lap of protection still hungered for the drama of violence. They became spectators of violence and bloodsport. Gladiators fought each other to the death to entertain the Roman tribe, and the people crowded into massive stadiums like the Circus Maximus to watch chariot races highlighted by gory wrecks. There were chariot racing "color" gangs who brawled after the events like today's soccer hooligans. Political figures, landowners, and merchants employed gangs of armed young men to intimidate their opponents, tenants, and business rivals.

Rome was founded by a gang, and it behaved like a gang. To paraphrase St. Augustine, it acquired territory, established a base, captured cities, and subdued people. Then it openly arrogated itself the title of Empire, which was conferred on it in the eyes of the world, not by the renouncing of aggression but by the attainment of (temporary) impunity. Rome slowly collapsed from the inside as it became a giant, pointless, corrupt economic machine. The Roman machine, like the American economic machine, could no longer embody the virile ethos of the small bands of rebellious men responsible for its creation. Gangs of armed young men existed throughout its rise and fall, and there were gangs long after the glory of Rome was left in ruin.

The story of Rome is the story of men and civilization. It shows men who have no better prospects gathering together, establishing hierarchies, staking out land, and using strength to assert their collective will over nature, women, and other men.

A CHECK TO CIVILIZATION

What are men supposed to do when there's no land to settle and no one to fight?

One of the basic ideas of evolutionary psychology is that because human evolution occurred over a very long period of time, and then an explosion of technology thrust us into the modern world in a comparatively short period of time (recorded history), humans are more adapted physically and psychologically to the world as it *was* than they are to the world as it is today.

Our minds and bodies are adapted to function in a harder world. The situations that make us happy, depressed or afraid have some sort of relationship to our ability to function in what some call the Environment of Evolutionary Adaptedness. The choices we make in the modern world may seem "illogical," but they reflect the kinds of choices we would have made to survive thousands of years ago. Think of all the time, energy, and resources we spend on sex even when we have no intention of reproducing. Logic's got nothing to do with it.

Our primal bodies and minds still make their calculations based on the old data. Maybe this is a bug, or maybe it's a feature—just in case shit goes down.

The first job of men has always been to keep the perimeter, to face danger, to hunt and fight. Men gather in bands and form a strong group identity. Men run through this pattern over and over again, whether it's logical or not.

Drawing on their understanding of primates, evolutionary biologists Richard Wrangham and Dale Peterson came up with a theory about male gang behavior they dubbed, perhaps unflatteringly, *male demonism.*

> "Demonic males gather in small, self-perpetuating, self aggrandizing bands. They sight or invent an enemy "over there"—across the ridge, on the other side of the boundary, on the other side of a linguistic or social or political or ethnic or racial divide. The nature of the divide hardly seems to matter. What matters is the opportunity to engage in the vast and compelling drama of belonging to the gang, identifying the enemy, going on the patrol, participating in the attack."[50]

Calling this phenomenon "demonism" puts an immoral spin on our species' basic survival strategy. It's a strategy that worked for us for a very long time, and a strategy that we'd snap back to in an emergency.

But, once you've founded Rome...what then?

Sometimes there is a good reason to make war, to identify *them* and mobilize *our men* against *theirs*. Sometimes there isn't. Every generation of young men can't be guaranteed a great crisis or war simply to give them an opportunity to explore their "demonic" primal nature or give their lives a sense of meaning. Starting wars for the sake of narrative seems frivolous, though I wonder if we do it subconsciously...out of sheer boredom. Sometimes men pick fights just for something to do—just to *feel* something like the threat of harm and the possibility of triumph.

Most of the time, men seek out substitutes for fighting. In tribal societies, this was probably easy enough. Hunting is something like fighting, and that's why men still do it even though they don't have to. Play fighting—sparring—is part of learning to fight, and men ritualize play fighting with sport.

In 1906 William James called for a "moral equivalent of war." Putting aside the question of whether war is moral or immoral, the phrase "moral equivalent of war" captures our need to suppress and redirect primal masculinity in peacetime. James acknowledged that men seemed to be perpetually in want of some "campaigning" way of life. As a pacifist, he suggested that all young men be drafted for a certain period in a "war against nature" where they could toil and suffer together as fishermen, coal miners, road-builders, and so forth.

The idea of a war on nature wouldn't play very well today, but if it were tweaked a bit, it might be the most honest and realistic way to reimagine masculinity. James laughed at the now-vindicated fears of his contemporaries who believed that without a sufficiently warlike nationalism, the United States would degenerate into a society, "of clerks and teachers, of co-education and zoo-ophily, of consumer's leagues and associated charities, of industrialism unlimited, and feminism unabashed." However, he also warned that "a permanently successful peace-economy cannot be a simple pleasure-economy."[51]

William James' plan for peace might have worked for a while, though I doubt any plan for peace is viable in the long term. The problem with outlawing violence is that doing so requires violence, and the problem with outlawing war is that doing so requires universal simultaneous agreement to outlaw war—otherwise, the peaceful doves end up sitting ducks.

Whether it would have worked or not, men were never shipped off to fight a war against nature—but we still keep ourselves engaged with "equivalents" of war. Like energy, gang masculinity isn't created or destroyed. This "demonism" is part of what men are and what they've evolved to do. It's always there; it just takes on different forms.

If a civilization is to grow and prosper, the tendency of men to break into gangs becomes an internal security threat. Gangs of men always pose a threat to established interests. "Equivalents" of gang masculinity have the potential to keep men invested in a given society and to keep them from tearing it apart. Viable substitutes for the masculine "campaigning way of life" keep men from asserting their own interests over the interests of the whole, or of those in power.

When men are materially invested in a society—when they believe there is more of what they want to gain by working for the group than by working against it—men will control and redirect their energies in the service of a prosperous society.

When men are emotionally invested in a society—when they feel a strong connection to the group, a strong sense of us— men will control and redirect their energies in the service of a peaceful society as long as the most aggressive men (the men who are better at being men) are provided with desirable "equivalents" to gang aggression.

As prosperity and security increase, and the need for men to hunt, struggle and fight decreases, the male desire to engage in gang activity can be controlled and channeled through simulation, vicariousness, and intellectualization.

Simulated Masculinity

- Primal gang aggression and gang bonding are directly simulated through participation in military service, police service, and similar "guardian" activities.

- Primal gang aggression and gang bonding are experienced through participation in ritualized and symbolic gang activities like team sports or cooperative gaming.

- Primal aggression, competitiveness, and the need to prove masculinity to the group are channeled through participation in individual sports, survival games, or individual competitions that require demonstrations of strength, courage, or mastery.

Vicarious Masculinity

- Males watch other males participate in wars, guardian work, and survival games.

- Males watch other males participate in team or individual sports.

- Males watch other males demonstrate strength, courage, mastery, or honor.

- Males study the history of males who participated in wars, guardian work, survival games, who participated in team or individual sports, or who have demonstrated strength, courage, mastery, or honor.

- Males read literature and stories about males who participate in wars, guardian work, and survival games, who participate in team or individual sports, or who have demonstrated strength, courage, mastery, or honor.

- Males watch films or plays about males who participate in wars, guardian work, and survival games, who participate in team or individual sports, or who have demonstrated strength, courage, mastery, or honor.

Intellectualized Masculinity

Economic aggression and gang activity – men or groups of men compete to outwit each other through economic competition. They demonstrate strength and courage by testing each other to see who is going to back down first and who is going to press his interests furthest. One example is a commissioned salesman selling an automobile to an informed buyer. Economic masculinity is demonstrated by taking risks and believing that you are competent enough to prevail. Companies benefit from intellectualized masculinity when men are more productive because they are encouraged to compete against each other.

Political/ideological aggression and gang activity – men form political or ideological teams and compete to win debates and battles of wit and strategy. Examples include political strategy, philosophical debate, academic or scientific debate, religious debate, and the guys who spend hours on message boards and comment threads trying to prove they are right about almost anything.

Metaphorical masculinity – for religious, ideological, or personal reasons, men turn masculinity inward. External battles become metaphors for internal battles, and the focus is on self-mastery, impulse control, disciplined behavior and perseverance. Men struggle to be good men, to be rational men, to be good fathers, to be good citizens, to be faithful men, to invent and create, to achieve goals.

Ascetic masculinity – the self-mastery and self-discipline of metaphorical masculinity leads to a tunneled focus on self-denial and the rejection of natural male desires for sex, food, worldly things, virile action, or violence.

I first envisioned simulated, vicarious, and intellectual masculinity as a progression running in one direction. My thinking was that as societies become safer and more prosperous, masculinity is simulated, then mostly vicarious, then mostly intellectualized. That makes some sense in the very big picture, but it doesn't work exactly like that.

Most or all of these substitutes for gang masculinity have been present in every kind of social organization and civilization. There have almost always been sports, and men who enjoyed watching sports and other contests of strength, speed, or agility. Primitive and civilized peoples alike have told stories of great deeds and reflected on what it meant to be a good man. Humans have been trading and negotiating for a long time, and there have almost always been priests and monks and ascetics.

Further, most or all of these methods of channeling gang masculinity can be present in and important to any given man. There are and have always been pious warriors and athletes. Manly men are generally expected to be good men, to exercise self-restraint, and to behave ethically. Men who we see as men of action will still take political sides or debate with one another. Men who play sports usually enjoy watching them. Overcoming internal struggles is essential to overcoming external struggles, to surviving, and to achieving anything.

So, both individual men and civilizations can and do channel masculinity through simulation, vicariousness, and intellectualization at any point in their development. What changes is emphasis and opportunity.

Because gangs are a threat to order unless they are organized in the service of a civilization, opportunities for the direct experience of gang masculinity—participation in war-making, protecting, and defending—will generally be available to a smaller proportion of the male population as the big gang that runs the civilization through one means or another "attains impunity." Some men will fight, but fewer. Modern technology speeds this up. If you have the ability to attack safely and *indirectly* with remote drones, few men will ever have to kill anyone *directly*.

The plenty produced by modern technology also reduces the opportunity for men to engage in "wars on nature," as James put it. Fewer and fewer men will be required to work actively with their hands as they would have in a primitive survival gang. Agriculture will replace group hunting, and machine-driven agribusiness or state-run agriculture will turn the trade of farming into a low-skill "job" that requires no emotional investment from men. Hunting gives way to the conveyor-belt slaughterhouse, and the efficiency of that system ensures that even fewer men will be required to participate in the hunting process. Hunting survives for most men only as a sport. We get our meat from the supermarket. For most of us today, what we do to get the money to buy the meat has little or nothing to do with hunting. It doesn't have to happen this way, but it has.

As *opportunities* for men to do what they evolved to do decrease, greater *emphasis* is placed on simulated, vicarious, and intellectualized channels of masculinity to maintain order and cultural unity. Men still get to feel like men, but the threat that men pose to order, to established interests, and to the interests of women is mitigated.

Men compete for status, and they want to earn peer approval, so the channels for masculinity that appeal to them will be related to their natural aptitudes and temperament. Guys with thin frames and high metabolisms may not make the best powerlifters, but they usually make good runners. Likewise, intellectuals and verbally gifted men take especially well to intellectualized channels of masculinity.

Most men are talented evenly enough that they can remain engaged by a mix of simulated, intellectualized, and vicarious forms of masculinity so long as they are otherwise invested in a given civilization.

A minority of men need extremely frequent opportunities for vital, immediate equivalents to hunting and war as they can get to keep them productive, and to keep them from self-destructing. Charles Darwin thought that these "restless" men were a "great check to civilization" but that they could "make useful pioneers."[52] These men tend to get into a lot of trouble in higher civilizations—they fill our prisons and often have problems with substance abuse—whereas they'd probably do pretty well in a survival scenario.

Another small number of men are happy to live almost completely in their heads, and are easily satisfied by intellectual pursuits and abstract demonstrations of masculinity. Just as jocks brag that real men play sports because they are good at them, abstract thinkers will pretend they have conquered their baser instincts by simply doing what they are naturally good at. Men compete for status, and they want to feel like they are winning.

Once you recognize this, debates between men about the true nature of masculinity become amusingly predictable. Engineers think manhood is all about technology, liberal arts majors think it is about civilized virtue, and athletes think masculinity is all about strength, speed, and perseverance. Effeminate males think they are more "evolved" than their brutish brothers, and thus, the truly better men. In a balanced, unified, patriarchal society that provides opportunities for the majority of men to put their talents to use, all of those guys can be right—at least partially. They can all demonstrate strength, courage, mastery, and honor to their peers in different ways, and they can all feel valued by a set of peers. Ideally, those guys could cultivate a modicum of respect for their different roles—though since status-seeking is the way of men, men with healthy egos will usually believe that their own role is just a little more important, and a little bit better.

Unfortunately, we've reached a level of civilization, technology, and plenty that—to protect order and established interests—opportunities for vital, immediate equivalents to hunting and war are increasingly rare. Weapons technology has made war too deadly and too easy for men willing to use that technology to get what they want at all costs. Lawyers and insurance companies—and more technology—have made dangerous, exciting, and engaging jobs safe, easy, and boring. Only a select few guardians, workers in shrinking and outsourced fields and men who favor intellectual channels of masculinity are satisfactorily engaged in activities where they feel like they are risking, struggling, and winning. Everyone else is just playing around, and they know it. Men are dropping out and disengaging from our slick, easy, safe world. For what may be the first time in history, the average guy can afford to be careless. Nothing he does really matters, and—what's worse—there is a shrinking hope of any future where what he does will matter.

Pornography is not the same as sex. It's a substitute for it. Would pornography lose its appeal without the possibility of sex? Will war and survival simulations be enough without even the remotest possibility of war or strife? Will they simply become empty, depleting, and depressing?

This is one reason why people love zombie movies and "disaster porn" so much. The apocalypse—any apocalypse—offers an opportunity. As the back cover of *The Walking Dead* comic book reads, "In a world ruled by the dead, we are forced to finally start living."

The compromise between modern civilization and manliness promoted by intellectuals is, predictably, an increased emphasis on intellectualized channels for masculinity. There are a few problems with this.

For starters, not all men are intellectuals, so they are going to suck at that game. No one likes losing all the time—ask any nerd or fag who has been bullied. If only a minority of men are intellectuals, and intellectualized masculinity is all we have, the majority of men are going to feel like they are losing all the time. If you want to create a society of listless antisocial losers, convince the majority of your men that they're already losing, and that no matter what they do, they will never be able to win.

What's the point in trying if you know the game is rigged?

For the satisfaction of knowing you are contributing to the greater good?

That's just the kind of stupid thing an intellectual would say.

Another problem with the complete intellectualization of masculinity is that intellectualized masculinity is pretty much equally accessible to women. Demonstrating your manliness to other men doesn't mean much if women are doing all of the same things that men are doing. "Intellectual courage" isn't particularly specific to men or the role of men. Women can be equally "intellectually courageous." Women can screw each other over in business just as well as men can—maybe even better. Women can demonstrate self-mastery. They can be good citizens. Women can be morally upright, and while as a group they lag in the sciences, there are women who can compete with men in every academic field. Intellectualized masculinity is only workable when masculinity is intellectualized differently than femininity and men are not forced to compete with women. If men are subconsciously trying to demonstrate their worthiness as men to other men, and then find themselves competing with women, it kind of blows the whole illusion.

The introduction of women into a field of competition short-circuits its viability as a substitute for male gang activity.

Competition doesn't satisfy the same primal need in most men when women are involved—no matter how the women behave, or how rational the reason for including them may seem. As a general rule, if you introduce women into the mix, men either shift their focus from impressing each other to impressing the women, or they lose interest altogether and do just enough to get by.

Feminist demands for absolute equality and the integration of the sexes into war and its equivalents—combined with the looming threat of technological mass destruction and the desire of globalist elites to protect their investments against ornery gangs of men—have pushed the intellectualization of masculinity into a terminal phase: **repudiation**. Accepting the nature of men as it is and offering them equivalents to war is no longer acceptable to women or globalists. Their shared agenda has become the complete repudiation of the idea that men should want to do the things they've been selected to do.

Boys are scolded even for their violent fantasies—for the violent stories they want to hear, the violent books they want to read, the violent games they want to play. Male "demonism" is punished, pathologized, and stigmatized from cradle to campus. Even the good guys are treated like bad guys for ganging up, for being "xenophobic," patriotic, or too exclusive. Video games, fighting sports, and movies are decried for being "too violent." Football is deemed "too dangerous" by many overprotective parents. Everyone is supposed to agree that violence is never the answer—unless that violence comes from the cutting edge of the State's axe.

Only those natural ascetics and intellectuals will truly be satisfied by the repudiation of gang masculinity as a substitute for gang masculinity. For most men, this repudiation of the role of men and our species' basic survival strategy will feel—rightly—like self hatred and oppression. The Way of Men is to gang up and fight each other, or fight nature. Teaching men to despise that is teaching them to despise their history, to hate their own talents and to reject their natural place in the world.

The repudiation of violent masculinity is the murder of male identity.

It's handicapping them and condemning them to a life of losing by cutting off their best chance at winning. Cultural repudiation of The Way of Men extinguishes the dream of virile action and makes its equivalents seem hollow and base. It erases the secret hope of men—the fantasy that one day they will be tested, that one day they will be thrust into a dire world at the bloody edge between life and death where everything they do will really matter.

In a recent column for *Asia Times*, Spengler argued that cultures facing their own imminent demise implode or lash out. They operate under a different standard of rationality, like a man who has been diagnosed with a terminal illness. Our modern idea of rational behavior fails to comprehend that kind of spiritual crisis. He wrote:

> "Individuals trapped in a dying culture live in a twilight world. They embrace death through infertility, concupiscence, and war. A dog will crawl into a hole to die. The members of sick cultures do not do anything quite so dramatic, but they cease to have children, dull their senses with alcohol and drugs, become despondent, and too frequently do away with themselves. Or they may make war on the perceived source of their humiliation."[53]

The restless men who sense that they will never be pioneers—who will never build the fire, keep watch over the camp or fight for their lives—may turn out to be the check of civilization. Look at what hopeless, directionless, angry young black men have done to the cities that were never theirs. See how well the once-proud Aztecs reacted to the rape of their cities and foreign rule. White men are equally capable of bringing down a future they have no place in—a future built on dreams that are not their own.

The emotional needs of men are not being met by a world that repudiates The Way of Men, but so long as their material needs are being met, men may choose not to make war against the world. As long as they have enough stuff, enough food, enough distractions—men may be content to dull their senses, tune out, and allow themselves to become slaves to the interests of women, bureaucrats, and wealthy men.

THE BONOBO MASTURBATION
SOCIETY

What would happen if men got spoiled, gave up, and gave in to women completely? How would that society operate?

The evolutionary theory of parental investment suggests that because reproduction is costly, members of the sex which makes the lesser parental investment will compete for sexual access to whichever sex makes the greater parental investment. In humans and most mammals, females are forced to make the greatest investment in reproduction.

Human females carry their children for nine months, and they are highly vulnerable and less mobile during the later stages of pregnancy. Giving birth itself is traumatic, and death during childbirth was more common in the past than it is today. After birth, the mother remains especially vulnerable for a short period, and a human child is extremely vulnerable for several months, and will remain vulnerable for several years. Nursing is another investment required of human mothers until recently.

Human males have it comparatively easy. We can pass on our genes in a matter of minutes, and then skip town unless we are persuaded to stick around by females, social controls or shotgun-wielding fathers.

Human males evolved to compete for access to females because female reproductive investment is a valuable prize. Males can exist in the all-male world of the gang, but females quite literally represent the future. Men create a perimeter and establish security. They create a rudimentary hierarchy, order, and seminal culture of us vs. them. To perpetuate the us, they need women. So they try to figure out how to get women, and how to get "access to their reproductive investment."

Major West, a character in the zombie movie *28 Days Later*, tells a story reminiscent of the founding of Rome. He gives the rationale for the rape of the Sabine women in just a few lines:

> "Eight days ago, I found Jones with his gun in his mouth. He said he was going to kill himself because there was no future. What could I say to him? We fight off the infected or we wait until they starve to death... and then what? What do nine men do except wait to die themselves? I moved us from the blockade, and I set the radio broadcasting, and I promised them women. Because women mean a future."[54]

The Way of Men is the Way of The Gang, but a gang of men, alone, has no future. The all-male gang ends with the death of the last man. Men want to be remembered, they want their tradition to survive, and they want sex. Ultimately, these psychological mechanisms and desires will allow them to pass on their genes. When there is competition for resources—including women—it is good strategy for a gang of men to create a patriarchal hierarchy, eliminate neighboring rival gangs, take their women, and protect the women from rival gangs. This is exactly what many primitive tribes do. This is the basic strategy of the gang.

What happens when competition for resources is radically

reduced?

What happens when women get *their* way?

Two of our closest primate relatives, chimpanzees and bonobos, illustrate some of the differences between the way of males and the way of females.

Wrangham and Peterson argued that in spite of cultural determinist theories and a lot of wishful thinking about peaceful pre-historic matriarchies—the evolutionary, archaeological, historical, anthropological, physiological, and genetic evidence overwhelmingly suggests that humans have always been a patriarchal, male-bonded party-gang species that engaged in regular coalitionary violence. This was a brave conclusion, because both authors seemed to be whole-heartedly against violence. As self-described evolutionary feminists, they offered suggestions as to how we might end male violence now that men have the means to wreak havoc well beyond what their primitive ancestors could do with powerful arms and simple tools. Aside from selective breeding to reduce violent alpha tendencies in males—a program that seems to be underway, albeit accidentally—and the establishment of one-world government, Wrangham and Peterson suggested that we look to the gentle bonobo apes for guidance.

Chimpanzees and bonobos are both close relatives of humans. Both have much in common with people, but when it comes to social structures, the chimps are more apt to live in small groups led by a hierarchical gang of males, whereas the bonobos tend to live in larger, more stable parties with a greater number of females and the females maintain coalitions that check male violence. Chimpanzees organize to the benefit of male reproductive interests, and bonobos organize to the benefit of female reproductive interests. Chimps follow The Way of Men. Bonobos follow The Way of Women.

The Chimpanzee Way

Chimpanzees can mingle in larger parties if they are able to make alliances, and if food is plentiful. Chimps and humans prefer high-quality foods, and male chimps actively hunt for meat, especially red colobus monkeys. Chimpanzees compete for resources when they are scarce, so they break up into smaller gangs. This is a "party-gang" social structure because of this flexibility in party size. Under stress, they revert to patriarchal gangs run by male relatives and bonded male allies. Females move (and are moved) from gang to gang. Males compete for sexual access to females, but males also sometimes court the females and escort them away from the stress of male competition. Females who do not have children sometimes join males in hunting and raiding activities. Females are subordinate to males in the chimpanzee social hierarchy, and they are expected to demonstrate submission. When a young male comes of age, he will usually make a big show of it and start pushing females around until they acknowledge him as an adult male. After he achieves that, he'll stop making such a big to-do. However, chimpanzee males do batter females sporadically to maintain their status and show the gals what's what. Males who come of age spend a lot of time together, but also spend a lot of time competing for status with each other. Their contests are often violent, and on rare occasions, two males have been known to form an alliance and murder the alpha male. Humans might recognize this as patricide or tyrannicide. For chimps, in-group competition is less important than competition with other groups. Chimpanzees and humans are the only two members of the great apes where males form coalitions to go out and raid or eliminate members of a neighboring gang. Alpha chimps will occasionally gather up other males, go out to the edge of their range, try to catch a member of another gang unaware, and murder him. This is similar to the "skulking way of war" common among primitive humans, who also engage in guerilla raiding.[55] Over time, males will pick off all of the other males of the neighboring gang, absorb the remaining females into their own group, and mate with them. Because chimpanzees hunt, defend and aggress as a coordinated gang, they have to be willing to put aside internecine competition and maintain close bonds with each other. Primatologist Frans de Waal wrote:

> "...the chimpanzee male psyche, shaped by millions of years of intergroup warfare in the natural habitat, is one of both competition and compromise. Whatever the level of competition among them, males count on each other against the outside. No male ever knows when he will need his greatest foe. It is, of course, this mixture of camaraderie and rivalry among males that makes chimpanzee society so much more recognizable to us than the social structure of the other great apes."[56]

The Bonobo Way

Bonobos eat many of the same foods that chimpanzees like, and they will eat meat when they find it. However, bonobos don't share their territory with gorillas, so they are able to eat the kinds of portable herbs that gorillas eat. Wrangham and Peterson believe that this is one of the key differences between chimps and bonobos. Bonobos have a staple food source that is easy to find. They don't have to compete for resources even when many foods are out of season, so they can more or less relax all year long in a peace of plenty. The males compete for status, but they seem less concerned about it because status for bonobo males doesn't mean much. Bonobos don't compete for mates. Each male just waits his turn, and the females are happy to oblige anyone who comes knocking. For the bonobos sex is social, and bonobos have both homosexual and heterosexual sex. Bonobo males don't know who their kids are because any of the kids could be their kids. The mother makes all of the parental investment. Bonobo males do know who their mothers are, and they remain bonded to them for life—they often follow their mothers around throughout adulthood, and mothers intervene in conflicts on behalf of their sons. Males don't spend a lot of time together in bonobo groups, but females build strong friendships with one another. When males start trouble, the females band together to put a stop to it quickly. Bonobo females are in charge. When one group of bonobos comes in contact with another group, the female bonobos will be the ones who make the peace, and generally, they will start engaging in hoka-hoka with each other—that's what natives call bonobo girl-on-girl action. Then the females will start mating with the males from the opposite group. The males just sit around and watch, shrug their shoulders, and eventually join in.

A Conflict of Interests

Bonobos and chimpanzees are adapted to different environments, and their social structures follow from what those environments have to offer. Bonobo society favors female interests. Female coalitions hold sway over politics, and female bonding is more important than male bonding. Males are bonded to their mothers and don't know who their fathers are. Females stay together for life. In chimpanzee society, females are somewhat isolated and stay with their young when they are children, while males enjoy both rivalry and camaraderie, and stay with their fathers, brothers, and male friends for life. Chimpanzee society favors male interests.

Wrangham and Peterson believe that bonobos offer a "threefold path to peace" because they have managed to reduce violence between the sexes, reduce violence between males, and reduce violence between communities.[57] In response to the mass destruction inherent to modern warfare, many men have searched for ways to abandon the "warfare system"[58] that attends patriarchy, and they have looked to women for guidance on coalition building and finding a more peaceful way to live.

Those who believe human warfare is somehow unnatural will find little objective support for this theory in history or the sciences. Human societies are complex, and aspects of both bonobo and chimpanzee patterns are familiar enough. But male aggression, male coalitional violence, and male political dominance have all been identified as "human universals"—meaning that evidence of these behaviors have been found in some form in almost every human society that has ever been studied.[59]

Scientists only began to study bonobos as a separate and distinct species in the 1950s, because bonobos evolved in a small, sheltered range. Chimpanzees have a much larger range, and have adapted to more diverse environments. Humans and chimps clearly have more in common in terms of social organization. It is likely that while humans are smarter and have far more complex social arrangements than chimpanzees, male bonding and male coalitional violence have been constant features of human and pre-human societies.

The following table shows the differences between various aspects of chimpanzee societies and bonobo societies—it shows two ways, two extremes.

MALE INTERESTS VS. FEMALE INTERESTS

	Male Interests (Chimpanzees)	**Female Interests** (Bonobos)
Resources	Variable, sometimes difficult to obtain	Readily available
Hunting Priority	High	Low
Male Alliances	Yes	No
Female Alliances	No	Yes
Sexuality	For mating	For socialization and pleasure
Homosexuality	Minimal, uncommon	Frequent, common
Political Dominance	Males	Shared, but female coalitions have most influence
Males -- Parent Bonding	Father, Brothers, patrilineal Males spend time with mothers during youth, with other males for the rest of their lives, with females for mating	Mothers, matrilineal, generally stay in party
Males Batter Females	Yes	No
Males Rape Females	Yes, but rare	Why bother?
Females acknowledge male dominance	Yes	No
Range Defended	Yes	Sometimes
Intergroup Raiding	Yes	No
Border Patrols	Yes	No

Some researchers have suggested that bonobos aren't as peaceful as Wrangham and Peterson believed, but it does seem clear that they are more peaceful and matriarchal than chimps, and that their lifestyle is similar to what I've described.

As a metaphor for what happens to men living in a secure peace of plenty like our own, the bonobo way looks eerily familiar.

Aren't most men today spoiled mamma's boys without father figures, without hunting or fighting or brother-bonds, whose only masculine outlet is promiscuous sex?

Wars against men are known to fewer and fewer of us. Mandatory conscription for the Vietnam War ended the year before I was born. Since then, the United States has effectively created a class of professional contract soldiers who do the government's fighting in faraway lands. Average men know more about collegiate basketball than they know about a given overseas conflict.

Like the bonobos, we don't have to worry about hunger. We barely have a reason to get up off the couch. Until the recent extended recession, jobs were fairly easy to come by, and almost all of the men who wanted to work were able to get a job. Welfare and social assistance programs provide safety nets for many others, and few American men living today grew up in a home without a television. True hunger and poverty and desperation, the way people know it in Africa, is rare even for those who are officially considered poor. Diseases that wiped out populations in the past are treatable, and people recover fully from injuries that would have been fatal one hundred years ago. If anything illustrates the surreal plenty we live in today, it is the fact that we have problems like epidemic obesity. People are able to sit in their homes and eat until they are so fat they can't move.

Americans are obese in part because they simply don't *do* enough. It's hard to find a job doing the kind of back-breaking work our ancestors did. I know, because I'm the kind of person who thinks a temp job digging ditches sounds like fun. *I've actually looked.* Our bodies have a tremendous capacity for work when we are conditioned for it. The human body is made to work hard. When there is no work to do, our physical health deteriorates. Doctors have to tell people to walk like it is some kind of breakthrough exercise technology. Once, I watched in awe as a personal trainer authoritatively led a pair of forty-something adults on a walk around their own neighborhood. He was a seventy-five dollar an hour human dog-walker.

The rest of us go to the gym to "work out," which is just a substitute for doing physical work. People who answer emails for a living go to a special building where they trick their bodies into thinking they are actually doing the kind of work humans evolved to do. Activities like sandbag training and stone lifting and barefoot running are becoming popular. It's only a matter of time before someone comes up with a way to market a fitness craze where people run around spearing rubber mammoths.

The goal of civilization seems to be to eliminate work and risk, but the world has changed more than we have. Our bodies crave work and sex; our minds crave risk and conflict.

It has always been striking to me that even in our most popular visions of the future, we have been unable to eliminate conflict. Take *Star Trek*, for instance. On the surface, *Star Trek* is a modernist, feminist, egalitarian dream. Men and women and people of all races work side-by-side in a one-world meritocracy that seeks peace across the universe. But our fantasy isn't the peace: it's the conflict. Without some conflict between us and them, there is no plot. On *Star Trek*, they're always fighting someone. Many are attracted to peaceful platitudes like the ones heard in John Lennon's "Imagine," but people aren't actually very good, or very interested, in imagining a future without conflict. If someone wrote a sci-fi show without conflict, would anyone watch?

We are pretty good, however, at imagining inventive ways to masturbate our primal natures with "safe" virtual, vicarious, and abstract pleasures.

Our society has almost no tolerance for unsanctioned physical violence. Children are expelled from school for fighting, and something as historically common as a weaponless, drunken brawl can land men in court or in jail.

As coalitions of females, pandering politicians, and fearful men organize to child-proof our world, to ban guns and regulate violent sports, men retreat to redoubts of virtual and vicarious masculinity like video games and fantasy football because it's all they have left.

People are also seeking out other non-violent forms of simulated risk and "safe" adventure. From skydiving and bungee-jumping to guided mountaineering and adventure races, men and women are coming up with more and more ways to simulate the primitive human experience. Women and men have similar drives in different degrees, and what I've noticed while participating in 5Ks and CrossFit and the "Warrior Dash" is that after the novelty of it wears off, attendance often becomes increasingly female. While some women participate competitively, many more women enjoy these experiences socially and emotionally, stopping along the way to cheer and encourage their struggling sisters. I get the sense that many husbands and boyfriends recognize the masturbatory, "feel-good" nature of these activities and shrug their shoulders, wondering why they would run through the mud in ninety-degree heat *for no good reason*. From an evolutionary standpoint, it makes sense that women would tend to prefer and be more satisfied with "safe" and "fun" risk simulation, while men would long for real competition, real risk, and the potential of real status gains. The carefully orchestrated, sanitized, padded, insured and permitted exercise rarely compares to the fantasy of virile action and meaningful risk.

In video games, at least men experience *virtual* death.

As physical competition for resources has decreased, sex has become increasingly social, as it is for the bonobos. Men and women hook up to satisfy their primal drive to reproduce. To the chagrin of masculinity's reimaginers, women still respond sexually to the kinds of "alpha" traits and behaviors in men that would have made them good hunters and fighters. Displaying strength, courage, and mastery signals genetic superiority and high male status to women—even women who have no plans to reproduce. Men seek out women who appear to be hearty and fertile, and women trick men's monkey brains with lipstick, liposuction, and breast implants. Sex today is increasingly disconnected from mating, and for many, it has become a matter of "masturbating with someone else's body."

In many cases, what that body offers is a disappointment compared to the risk-free sex that men can have virtually and vicariously through immediately available, high-quality pornography. In 2003, feminist Naomi Wolf[60] and writer David Amsden[61] wrote that the simulated sexual experience was turning many men off to sex with real women, who felt that they had to compete with pornography for the attention of men.

2003...wasn't that back when people actually still paid for porn, and a gigabyte still sounded like a big file? Today young men can download high-definition pornography in moments and watch it on the same dazzling big-screen television that they bought to watch the Super Bowl. *New York Magazine* followed up in 2011 with a story titled "He's Just Not That Into Anyone," wherein the author reported faking an orgasm during real sex, but having no problems climaxing when watching porn. Some of the men he interviewed for the story told him that they were experiencing erectile dysfunction during real sex, and others told him they had to replay scenes from porn to get off while fucking their wives. Singer John Mayer confessed to Playboy magazine that there had probably been days where he had seen three hundred vaginas before getting out of bed.[62]

Our world isn't offering men more paths to virile fulfillment or vital experience.

What the modern world offers average men is a thousand and one ways to safely spank our monkey brains into oblivion.

Is it any wonder that some men ask themselves, in lucid moments between masturbating to various forms of vicarious sex and violence, what Betty Friedan wrote that educated housewives were asking themselves in the fifties:[63]

"Is this all?"

We were born into a peace of plenty, a pleasure-economy, a bonobo masturbation society.

The future that our elite handlers have in store for us advertises more of the same. More detached pleasure, less risk, freedom from want, more masturbation. Reimaginers of masculinity offer us metaphorical battles to fight, but in the real world the most meaningful battles will be "fought" between elite bureaucrats and experts and wealthy managers who believe they know what is best, while the rest of us shuffle off to boring, risk-free jobs to do idiot work and stare at the clock, waiting to go home and furiously indulge ourselves in whatever form of vicarious or virtual primitive experience gets us off.

Cosmopolitan journalists from elite schools like Betty Friedan filled women's imaginations with fantasies of exciting big-city careers that only a few could ever hope to attain. For every woman living that fantasy today, there are a bunch of women scanning merchandise through a checkout line at some big-box retail store, or doing repetitive data-entry in some gray office. In the East, women are answering our phone calls or performing monotonous assembly line tasks in factories. This is called "progress." Many of those women would probably rather be spending more time actively engaged in the lives of their children, but they no longer have the choice to stay home.

The cost of civilization is a progressive trade-off of vital existence. It's a trade of the real for the artificial, for the convincing con, made for the promise of security and a full belly.

It has always been so.

The question is: "how much trade is too much?"

In the future that globalists and feminists have imagined for themselves, only a few people will actually do anything worth doing. A few people will be scientists, charged with uncovering the mysteries of the universe. A few people will be engineers who dream and design and solve problems. A few people will inhabit a privileged managerial class of financiers and bureaucrats, and they will make all of the decisions that matter for everyone else. They will captain companies and departments and build their great Leviathans out of legal papers and fake smiles. There will also be, as there is now, a glamorous creative class charged with devising our sedentary entertainments. There will be gladiators and chariot races. There will be drama and theater people, and there will be global village gossip.

Still, everyone can't be a chief, and most of us will be Indians. Products need hordes of consumers and salespeople and customer service representatives and clerks and stock boys and loss prevention associates and midnight janitors. Anyone on the left-hand side of the bell curve, anyone who makes the wrong choices at the wrong time, anyone who doesn't jump through the hoops or play the game, anyone who hasn't been "properly socialized," and anyone who turns down the wrong options for the right reasons will end up doing those drone jobs. As Matthew B. Crawford observed in his book *Shop Class As Soulcraft*, even so-called white-collar "knowledge work" is "subject to routinization and degradation, proceeding by the same logic that hit manufacturing a hundred years ago: the cognitive elements of the job are appropriated from professionals, instantiated in a system or process, and then handed back to a new class of workers—clerks—who replace the professionals."[64] Being able to read and write at a college level doesn't mean the job you do will require much more thinking or consequential problem solving than you would have to do as a shift manager at McDonald's. It will only save you from the greasy forehead.

Only a couple hundred years ago, many of these men now destined for clerkdom would have learned a trade from their fathers and mastered it, whether it was farming or some other kind of engaging work that they could be proud of. They would have been valued members of a smaller community of people who cared whether they lived or died. Some would have spent their lives with gangs of men on ships, but most would have been bound to provide for and protect their families—their own small clans. This was a workable compromise between gang life and family life. A few generations ago, these men would have had meaningful responsibilities, and their actions would have had the potential to do more harm than merely hurting someone's feelings or causing them to be inconvenienced. They would have had pressing reasons to try to be good at being men, but also to be good men. Not so long ago, these men would have had dignity and honor.

In the future that globalists and feminists have imagined, for most of us there will only be more clerkdom and masturbation.

There will only be more apologizing, more submission, more asking for permission to be men. There will only be more examinations, more certifications, mandatory prerequisites, screening processes, background checks, personality tests, and politicized diagnoses. There will only be more medication. There will be more presenting the secretary with a cup of your own warm urine. There will be mandatory morning stretches and video safety presentations and sign-off sheets for your file. There will be more helmets and goggles and harnesses and bright orange vests with reflective tape. There can only be more counseling and sensitivity training. There will be more administrative hoops to jump through to start your own business and keep it running. There will be more mandatory insurance policies. There will definitely be more taxes. There will probably be more Byzantine sexual harassment laws and corporate policies and more ways for women and protected identity groups to accuse you of misconduct. There will be more micro-managed living, pettier regulations, heavier fines, and harsher penalties. There will be more ways to run afoul of the law and more ways for society to maintain its pleasant illusions by sweeping you under the rug. In 2009 there were almost five times more men either on parole or serving prison terms in the United States than were actively serving in all of the armed forces.[65]

If you're a good boy and you follow the rules, if you learn how to speak passively and inoffensively, if you can convince some other poor sleepwalking sap that you are possessed with an almost unhealthy desire to provide outstanding customer service or increase operational efficiency through the improvement of internal processes and effective organizational communication, if you can say stupid shit like that without laughing, if your record checks out, and your pee smells right—you can get yourself a J-O-B. Maybe you can be the guy who administers the test or authorizes the insurance policy. Maybe you can be the guy who helps make some soulless global corporation a little more money. Maybe you can get a pat on the head for coming up with the bright idea to put a bunch of other guys out of work and outsource their boring jobs to guys in some other place who are willing to work longer hours for less money. Whatever you do, no matter what people say, no matter how many team-building activities you attend or how many birthday cards you get from someone's secretary, you will know that you are a completely replaceable unit of labor in the big scheme of things.

No sprawling bureaucracy or global corporation can ever love you. They have public relations budgets and human resources departments to protect their interests and their bottom lines. There is no "us." A legal entity can't care if you live or die, or if you're happy.

If you're a good boy, if you're well-groomed and have a J-O-B, and you learn to say the right things, maybe you can convince a nice girl to let you give her a baby and help her pay for it. If that's not your thing, you can spend your money getting drunk or busy yourself trying to hump whatever piece of ass strikes your fancy. Sex, after all, is social in the bonobo masturbation society. You'll have the hard-won "right" to rub yourself against whatever makes you feel good, as long as you follow the rules.

If you're a good boy, you can curl up in the womb of your safe little Soviet-nouveau bloc apartment with your comfy stuff and enjoy your measured indulgences, your gourmet food, your microbrew. You can busy yourself trying to master the art of erasing your own carbon footprint, or you can do your part by biking to work, weaving recklessly through a barrage of trucks and cars that could crush you for the sheer thrill of it. Maybe you'll take a class and get your permit, and after another clerk confirms that you are competent enough to be licensed and properly insured, you'll be able to do something really crazy like ride a motorcycle. Maybe you'll pay someone to let you play a game or run a race or put on a safety harness and climb fake rocks. If not, you can always watch someone else do it on TV. Maybe you'll get yourself worked up about some petty inequity or injustice and participate in some non-violent resistance. Maybe you'll convince yourself that you are making a difference by standing in the same place with other people and shouting angrily at people who don't care. If you prefer, you can get online and vent your confused, impotent, vainglorious rage by playing the anonymous tough guy on some blog or forum. Or you can just say "fuck it" and spend all of your money on video games that give you the vicarious thrill of slaughtering hordes of aggressive "others." You can obsess over your fantasy football team. And there are always hobbies. You can find yourself something harmless and inoffensive to pass the time. Perhaps gardening. You can start a band or tinker with cars. Become a movie buff. You can paint little figurines of warriors. You can even get dressed up in costumes and do live-action role playing.

Whatever you do, just find some way to busy yourself.

There's nothing wrong with any of these things. All of them are "fun." What is "fun," if not masturbating your primal brain a little? I like having "fun." There's no harm in a little "fun," which is why it is called "fun"—and not something deadly serious, like "survival" or "war."

If that is all, if your life is all about chasing "fun," is that enough?

Is this level of civilization—is all of this peace and plenty—worth the cost?

How long will men be satisfied to replay and reinvent the conflict dramas of the past through books and movies and games, without the hope of experiencing any meaningful conflict in their own lives? When will we grow tired of hearing the stories of great men long dead?

How long will men tolerate this state of relative dishonor,

knowing that their ancestors were stronger men, harder men, more courageous men—and knowing that this heritage of strength survives in them, but that their own potential for manly virtue, for glory, for honor, will be wasted?

We know what The Way of Men has been.

Is the way of the bonobo the only way that is left?

Day after day, day after day,
We stuck, nor breath nor motion;
As idle as a painted ship
Upon a painted ocean.

—Samuel Taylor Coleridge

"Rime of the Ancient Mariner"

WHAT IS BEST IN LIFE?

The *Epic of Gilgamesh* is one of the earliest known works of literature, and it is the product of one of the earliest complex civilizations. It tells the story of Gilgamesh, a mortal man of tremendous natural strength and prowess. No man could stand against Gilgamesh until a goddess fashioned an equal for him named Enkidu—a wild hairy man of warlike virtue who "knew nothing of the cultivated land."

Enkidu was friends with the animals and ranged the countryside helping them, causing woe for trappers and shepherds in the area. The men conspired against him. They sent a naked harlot to tempt Enkidu and tell him of Gilgamesh and of wonders found in the luxurious city of Uruk so that Enkidu would leave the hills and stop threatening their livelihood. Enkidu was curious, and he longed for a friend who was his peer, another man who would understand him. He followed the harlot to the tents of the shepherds, and she clothed Enkidu and introduced him to bread and strong wine. He joined the shepherds and hunted wolves and lions for them. With Enkidu as their watchman, they prospered.

A man came to Enkidu and reminded him of Gilgamesh and the city of Uruk, where Gilgamesh was behaving like a tyrant. Enkidu decided to go to the city and challenge Gilgamesh. The two men fought each other, snorting and shattering doorposts and shaking the walls like two bulls. As they grappled, they gained respect for each other, and the two men decided to become friends.

Enkidu and Gilgamesh lived together in the city as brothers, but Gilgamesh was tormented by his own great potential and longed to do something that would be remembered. Enil, chief among the gods at that time, had given Gilgamesh "the power to bind and to loose, to be the darkness and the light of mankind." Enkidu complained to Gilgamesh that his own arms had grown weak, and that he was "oppressed by idleness." To fulfill their destinies, they knew they had to leave the comfort of the city and suffer and fight evil together. Gilgamesh cried out to the god Shamash:

> "Here in the city man dies oppressed at heart, man perishes
> with despair in his heart. I have looked over the wall and I
> see the bodies floating on the river, and that will be my lot
> also. Indeed I know it is so, for whoever is tallest among
> men cannot reach the heavens, and the greatest cannot
> encompass the earth. Therefore I would enter that country:
> because I have not established my name stamped on brick as
> my destiny decreed, I will go to the country where the cedar
> is cut. I will set up my name where the names of famous men
> are written; and where no man's name is written I will raise
> a monument to the gods.' The tears ran down his face and he
> said, 'Alas, it is a long journey that I must take to the Land
> of Humbaba. If this enterprise is not to be accomplished,
> why did you move me, Shamash, with the restless desire to
> perform it?"[66]

If there is a "crisis of masculinity," this is it, and the problem is as old as civilization itself.

The true "crisis of masculinity" is the ongoing and ever-changing struggle to find an acceptable compromise between the primal gang masculinity that men have been selected for over the course of human evolutionary history, and the level of restraint required of men to maintain a desirable level of order in a given civilization.

Civilized life and technology offer many benefits to men. The simple, hardscrabble lives of our primitive ancestors may not have been as nasty, brutish, or short as Hobbes believed, but it would be foolish to say that men have gained nothing from agricultural innovation or the division of labor. Without such changes, there would have been no great works of art or literature, no great buildings or monuments, no printing press, no laptop for me to type on. Countless people have died throughout history from infections that anyone can cure today with cheap over-the-counter medications. We enjoy abundant foods and strong, imported wines, and—perhaps most importantly—we have a steady supply of clean, drinkable water. Men wanted these things thousands of years ago when the *Epic of Gilgamesh* story was conceived.

Enkidu complained that he had grown weak and that he felt oppressed by the idleness of civilized life.

Men have known since Gilgamesh that civilization comes at a cost.

The manly virtues are raw and perishable. Males are, on average, naturally stronger, have a greater tendency to take risks, and they have a greater drive to master the world around them through technics—but all of these aptitudes require cultivation.

Muscles atrophy when improperly nourished and infrequently used. A man who never pushes his strength threshold will never even glimpse his physical potential, as anyone who has achieved substantial strength gains through physical training can attest. Strength is a "use it or lose it" aptitude.

Men may be natural risk-takers, but the increased confidence and surefootedness that we recognize as manly courage is the product of constant testing. The chest-thumping of untested men is hardly courage; Hobbes called it "vaine-glory", because "a well grounded confidence begetteth attempt; whereas the supposing of power does not."[67] Or, to put it in the words of Tyler Durden, "How much can you know about yourself, [if] you've never been in a fight?" Modern men are not merely lacking initiation into manhood, as some have suggested, they are lacking meaningful trials of strength and courage. Few modern men will truly "know themselves," as men, in the way that their forefathers did.

Likewise, skills must be mastered and practiced to be truly useful. Talent will only get you so far. If you are never truly challenged in a meaningful way and are only required to perform idiot-proofed corporate processes to get your meat and shelter, can you ever truly be engaged enough to call yourself alive, let alone a man?

Later in the *Epic of Gilgamesh*, after Gilgamesh killed the Bull of Heaven and overthrew the monstrous Humbaba, his comrade Enkidu died. Gilgamesh was distraught, and he searched for a way to cheat his own death. He met a young girl who made wine, and she told him that there was no way for him to avoid death. She told him to fill his belly with good things, to dance and be merry, to feast and rejoice. She told him to cherish his children and make his wife happy, "for this too is the lot of man."[68]

This *too*, is the lot of man.

In times of peace and plenty, when their bellies are full and they feel safe, women have always advised men to abandon manly pursuits and the way of the gang, to enjoy the safe pleasures of vicariousness and to join women in domestic life. When no threat is imminent, it has always been in the best interest of women to calm men down and enlist their help at home, raising children, and fixing up the grass hut. This is The Way of Women.

Men are people, too. It is not my intention to characterize men as soulless monsters who care about nothing but blood and glory. Men do love, sometimes more passionately and more unconditionally than women. Men can be tender and nurturing; any man who disputes that hates his father. Men write and tell stories and create things of remarkable beauty. All of these things can be part of being a man.

Men and women share much in common, but this book is not about the things that make men human; it is about the things that make them men.

Feminists dismiss biology and "outdated" ideas about masculinity and argue that men can change if they want to. Men do have free wills, and they can change to some extent, but men are not merely imperfect women. Men are individuals with their own interests, and they don't need women to show them how to be men. Women are not selfless spirit guides who have no interests or motivations of their own. Men have always had their own way, The Way of The Gang, and they've always inhabited a world apart from women.

"*Can* men change?" is the wrong question.

Better questions are: "Why *should* men change?" and "What does the average guy get out of the deal?"

When pressed to answer this question, feminists and men's rights activists never seem to be able to come up with anything but promises of increased financial and physical security and the freedom to show weakness and fear. Masses of men never rushed to the streets demanding the freedom to show weakness and fear, and they never braved gunfire or battle axes for the right to cry in public. Countless men, however, have died for the ideas of freedom and self-determination, for the survival and honor of their own tribes, for the right to form their own gangs.

Feminists, elite bureaucrats, and wealthy men all have something to gain for themselves by pitching widespread male passivity. The way of the gang disrupts stable systems, threatens the business interests (and social status) of the wealthy, and creates danger and uncertainty for women. If men can't figure out what kind of future they want, there are plenty of people who are ready to determine what kind of future they'll get.

They'll get a decorated cage.

They'll get a Fleshlight®, a laptop, a gaming console, a cubicle and a prescription drip.

They'll get some exciting new gadgets.

They'll get something that feels a little bit like being a man.

Women will continue to mock them, and they'll deserve it.

Lionel Tiger wrote that men "don't get what they're about not to have."[69] The world is changing, and men are being told that newer is always better, that change is inevitable, that the future feminists and globalists want is unavoidable. Men are being told that their future is logical, that it is moral, that it is better, and that men had better learn to like it. But who is this new world really better *for?*

Civilization comes at a cost of manliness. It comes at a cost of wildness, of risk, of strife. It comes at a cost of strength, of courage, of mastery. It comes at a cost of honor. Increased civilization exacts a toll of virility, forcing manliness into further redoubts of vicariousness and abstraction. Civilization requires men to abandon their tribal gangs and submit to the will of one big institutionalized gang. Globalist civilization requires the abandonment of the gang narrative, of us against them. It requires the abandonment of human scale identity groups for "one world tribe." The same kind of men who once saw their own worth in the eyes of the peers who they depended on for survival will have to be satisfied with a "social security number" and the cheerfully manipulative assurances of their fellow drones. Feminist civilization requires the abandonment of patriarchy and brotherhood as men have known it since the beginning of time. The future being dreamed for us doesn't require the reimaging of masculinity; it ultimately demands the end of manhood and the soft embrace of personhood that has long been the feminist prescription for this ancient crisis of masculinity.

This end of men, this decline of males, this new bonobo masturbation society of peace and plenty—this No Man's Land—is not inevitable. It will require the tacit or expressed consent of billions of men. Like every civilization, it must be built on the backs of men, and most of them must agree to abide by and enforce its laws. You can't have prisons without prison guards and you can't have security without some kind of police. Men will have to get up in the morning and go to their clerking jobs and smile and consume and continue to amuse themselves according to regulation. Civilization requires a social contract, and men have to keep up their end of the bargain for it to work.

This future can only happen if men help create it.

As I wrote in the opening chapter of this book, men must choose a way.

To make this choice, they must ask themselves:

"What is best in life?"

The "crisis of masculinity" poses exactly that philosophical question.

If you decide that true happiness for men lies in the elimination of risk, the satiation of hunger, the escape of labor, and the pursuit of "fun," then our bonobo future may sound like some kind of One World Las Vegas.

I have come to the conclusion that the lot of man is to find a balance between the domestic world of comfort and the world of manly strife. Men cannot be men—much less good or heroic men—unless their actions have meaningful consequences to people they truly care about. Strength requires an opposing force, courage requires risk, mastery requires hard work, honor requires accountability to other men. Without these things, we are little more than boys playing at being men, and there is no weekend retreat or mantra or half-assed rite of passage that can change that. A rite of passage must reflect a real change in status and responsibility for it to be anything more than theater. No reimagined manhood of convenience can hold its head high so long as the earth remains the tomb of our ancestors. Men must have some work to do that's worth doing, some sense of meaningful action. It is not enough to be busy. It is not enough to be fed and clothed and given shelter and safety in exchange for self-determination. Men are not ants or bees or hamsters. You can't just set up a plastic habitat and call it good enough. Men need to feel connected to a group of men, to have a sense of their place in it. They need a sense of identity that can't be bought at the mall. They need *us*, and to have *us*, you must also have *them*. We are not wired for "one world tribe."

I've been a non-believer all of my life, but I'd drop to my knees and sing the praises of any righteous god who collapsed this Tower of Babel and scattered men across the Earth in a million virile, competing cultures, tribes, and gangs.

Honor, as I understand the definition, requires that kind of "diversity."

I don't say this because I think I'd personally fare better in a more primitive society. I spent the last six months reading and writing, not training for the zombie apocalypse.

I hope that men, to quote Guy Garcia, "yank at their chains and pull the entire temple down with them,"[70] because I hate to think that this is the end of The Way of Men. Everyone from schoolteachers to the United Nations is rushing to do away with "outmoded" models of masculinity, but they're not replacing it with anything better. In a review of Steven Pinker's book about violence, James Q. Wilson mentioned that the real change occurs when men care more about getting rich than getting bloody.[71] It's tragic to think that heroic man's great destiny is to become economic man, that men will be reduced to craven creatures who crawl across the globe competing for money, who spend their nights dreaming up new ways to swindle each other. That's the path we're on now.

What a withering, ignoble end...

Humanity needs to go into a Dark Age for a few hundred years and think about what it's done.

"I prefer to not to use the words, 'let's stop something'.

I prefer to say, 'let's start something, let's start the world'."

—Peter Fonda, 2011

START THE WORLD

There is no democratic spur from our current path that can lead us back to The Way of Men.

The Men's Rights Movement seeks equity with women, and therefore points in the same direction as feminism. It wants to relieve men of making sacrifices on behalf of women. It wants men and women alike to pursue individual prosperity without special, gendered obligations or clearly defined sex roles. The anger that drives the Men's Rights Movement comes from a sense that women aren't playing fairly, that they are cheating, that when given the chance, they will use the rhetoric of equality to skew things in their own favor. The men are right about that. Women are re-designing the world in their own image. It is naïve for men to expect otherwise.

The Way of Men is to fight the external threat, and to fight other men. Sometimes men fight *over* women, but men have no history of fighting women. During times of peace and plenty it has always been the Way of Women to lure men to away from the volatile gang, to seek his investment in her reproductive endeavor, and to encourage him to seek refuge and comfort in domesticity. A comfortable man is less likely to take risks, and warriors have always known that too much comfort makes men soft. Men are not going to rise up and form one great political action committee to fight the influence of women. Men of means see too much immediate social and financial gain in catering to the interests of women. Politicians see a more politically and socially active population that must be appeased, and they will continue to fall all over themselves to get the female vote. Women are better suited to and better served by the globalism and consumerism of modern democracies that promise security, no-strings-attached sex, and shopping. For the most part, male bureaucrats cannot be counted on to help men who they don't know, when there is a political risk involved. Again, it is naïve for men to expect otherwise.

Another bulwark to social change on behalf of men is the reality of globalism. In America, we are conditioned to think of corporations as "The Man," but that's a very Twentieth Century sense of things. Today's robber-barons and fat cats are figureheads that captain global enterprises which can basically function without them. The reigning presidents and CEOs are often as disposable as the workers. They come and go. There is no "Man." There is only the profit-driven, hydra-headed legal entity, whose workers make cost/benefit analyses to increase profit and further their own status and salary, usually with an eye on producing immediate, short-term results. Those workers don't care about what happens to a company in ten years, because if they are savvy and career-minded, they may well be working for a competitor by then. There is no "conspiracy" here, only people looking out for their immediate interests. If the legal department fears legal action, it will go through human resources and pre-empt it by initiating anti-sexist or anti-racist policies, or even soft affirmative action and public relations programs that reach out to litigious communities.

It is in the interest of corporate enterprises in most cases to champion anti-sexist (pro-feminist) and anti-racist policies because identity conflicts can be costly and inefficient. To the global corporation, people are interchangeable units of labor priced at different values. Your sexual or tribal identity is a nuisance and a source of potential liability. Only thin identities are advantageous—like the kind of music or movies you prefer. Thin identities are marketing niches. *Us* vs. *them* identities and different sex roles are problematic and cumbersome. But don't take my word for it; I'm a right-wing sexist. America's favorite left-wing anarchist, Noam Chomsky, wrote that "Capitalism basically wants people to be interchangeable cogs" and that differences among them are "usually not functional."[72] Chomsky was talking about race, but his comments that corporations see people only as "consumers and producers" and that "any other properties they might have are kind of irrelevant, and usually a nuisance" can logically be applied to differences between men and women. The genderless feminist utopia of humans who are neither masculine nor feminine is more efficient from the utilitarian perspective of the global enterprise. Don't expect the billions of dollars that international corporations wield to move in favor of men any time soon.

All of this is not to say that Men's Rights activists are wrong or useless, but that they can only perform triage and provide first aid. Men's Rights advocates can do things to make the situation better for men in the short term, like work for fairness in divorce proceedings and child custody cases and sexual harassment lawsuits. They can call attention to the lies and distortions of feminists, and they can work to discredit feminist "experts" on masculinity who repackage the same old 1970s boilerplate propaganda as "science" year after year. This is good work. Like what passes for conservatism today, it puts on a break that slows the degeneracy that feminists call "progress."

Women, individually, are not to blame for everything that has transpired over the past few hundred years. Individual women can certainly not be blamed for The Industrial Revolution. They can't be blamed for the trains, planes, and automobiles that make globalism possible. They can't be blamed for Marxism, or the birth control pill, or the Internet, or the shopping mall. Women, as a group, can probably be blamed for abominations like reality television, and for a lot of bad music and art, and for making mainstream magazines almost unreadably gossipy and stupid. But individual women, a few figureheads aside, can't fairly be blamed for a whole lot. Women are just acting according to their natures and skewing things in their interests, as they've always wanted to, and as men have prevented them from doing for most of human history. It's not as though men have been selfless creatures, historically speaking. Men and women alike can be tremendously generous and self-sacrificing, but on an average day, we'll take care of our own interests first. That's the Way of People.

The point of this book is not to portray women as evil shrews. Women are humans who are slightly different from men, and given the opportunity, they will serve their own slightly different interests and follow their own slightly different way. Women aren't evil, but they aren't angels, either. They are what they are. No matter how much sympathy some may have for the plight of modern men, women are not going to give up what they have so long as they believe it's worth having. They aren't going to rush to the polls to relieve themselves of advantages or support systems. As long as states offer women peace and plenty, women and big government will continue to enjoy a symbiotic relationship. Women can be sympathetic, but they're not dumb.

Any return to The Way of Men will fail to receive bipartisan support.

I also doubt that men will ever assert their interests as a sex through violent revolution. It's not realistic. There's no good pitch for it. Men aren't going to make the streets run red with their own blood for...well...what exactly would they even ask for? Men aren't going to rise up and storm the Capitol to demand the repeal of the Nineteenth Amendment. It would be easier to get them to riot in Washington D.C. to repeal the Sixteenth Amendment and end Federal Income Tax—something women could get on board with, too—and that isn't happening anytime soon. The closest thing they've managed in recent years was the Tea Party movement which, despite early media hysteria that it was a mob of angry white men, was quickly co-opted by women like Sarah Palin and Michelle Bachmann, who ended up turning it into something more like a tent revival potluck for heavily armed soccer moms.

Even if men were inclined to organize against the State in its current form, men would lose before they even started. The state has the ability to seek out and identify anti-state movements who plan to use violence, and has crushed organized armed resistance movements on numerous occasions. Men aren't dumb, either. Organized, armed resistance movements end in "death by cop" long before they gain the money, the numbers, or the momentum necessary to make themselves a viable threat. This ain't Africa or Central America.

But what if it were?

What if the United States were a little bit more like Mexico?

I worked with an illegal immigrant for a while, and he told me that while he loved his homeland and his culture, he didn't want to raise his family in a place without law and order. He told me stories about police shaking down drivers for cash instead of writing tickets. When I visited a border town a few years ago, it was striking how blurry the line was between the *Federales* and a gang. There was no "officer friendly." The *Federales* were a bunch of guys with assault rifles whose purpose was clearly to observe and intimidate. When they got a call, they jumped on the back of what looked like a Ford F150 with an aftermarket roll bar and made off in a cloud of desert dust. In other places, the *Federales* don't look so tough. It's not unusual for Mexican police to wear ski masks at work, for fear of gang retribution.[73]

That retribution can be brutal, as it was recently in the border town of Guadalupe, where a female police chief went missing around Christmas in 2010.

> "Erika Gandara was a former radio dispatcher for the police department in the town of 9,000, which is just across the U.S. border, one mile from Fabens, Texas. The previous police chief was murdered and decapitated; his head was found in an ice chest. Gandara, 28, a single woman with no children, was the only applicant for the job and its salary of $580 per month.
>
> One policeman was murdered during Gandara's first week on the job. By the time she became chief, the entire force of eight patrolmen had either been killed or fled. She was the sole law enforcement representative in a Juarez valley town that was part of the war between competing drug cartels for access routes into the U.S."[74]

In September 2011, *Reuters* reported that violence was slowing down in Tijuana after years of bloodshed, in part because the gangs there had finally settled a turf war, and one gang established near-complete control over the area.[75]

If men are going to re-assert their interests and return to The Way of Men, they're not going to do it through a democratic movement or a social movement or an armed political uprising. They're going to do it in a way that looks a lot more like what La Familia was doing with John Eldredge's work. They're going to do it through gangs in areas of the world where the State has lost power and credibility. They're going to take some of the ideas from surviving male traditions and repurpose them to create their own unique identities, their own us.

The current level of security we enjoy (or fear, depending on what side of the law you're on) is very, very expensive, and the United States is a very large territory. The quality of policing we have today is the direct result of our wealth and status as a major world power. Our police are on a payroll, and less money will mean fewer police, more frustrated police, and more police corruption. As the power of the State wanes, nonstate actors gain breathing room and influence. The United States is far bigger than North Korea, and the United States is not China. Mao had to kill over forty million people to get the Chinese on the same page. Not including those who died in various famines, it seems to have taken Stalin at least three million deaths to keep the Soviets in order. His tyranny gave birth to the Vory v Zakone, or "Thieves in Law," who represent only a small portion of the crime syndicates currently active in modern Russia.[76] Criminal gangs are active all over the United States, especially in border zones and ghettos where policing is inadequate or viewed as illegitimate and tyrannical, as it by many blacks who see the police as inherently racist, and in areas with high concentrations of illegal immigrants who see themselves as unfairly persecuted. For many, the State is already the "other."

In the film *Gran Torino*, Clint Eastwood's character Walt Kowalski confessed to Father Janovich that one of his "sins" was failing to pay taxes on a private sale he had made several years prior. He said, "It's the same as stealing." That's the country my grandfather lived in. Many people who grew up before the Vietnam era felt *that* connected to their nation. They were invested in it. The United States was us, or truer to the spirit of it, it was "we the people."

In the post-Vietnam era, it seems as though more and more people on the Left and the Right alike regard the government as "them." Whether they consider themselves Democrats, Republicans, or Independents of some kind, whether they make twenty thousand dollars a year or two hundred thousand dollars a year, most people today will pour over their tax returns looking for any way they can find to pay less. Few would give a second thought to claiming profits on a sale they've made using a craigslist ad. If you told them it was their civic duty, they'd probably give you the look they save for Jehovah's Witnesses. Small business owners usually find ways to cut corners, and many are happy to hide income or hire workers illegally or under the table to avoid paying taxes or dealing with complicated regulations. Every year average Americans download billions of dollars worth of pirated music and movies. Like smoking marijuana—the same pot that Mexican gangs are trafficking—these things have become socially acceptable practices at almost every level of society.

The Italians have a saying for this. *Tutti colpevoli, nessuno colpevole.*

It means, "If everyone is guilty, no one is guilty."

Walt Kowalski's America is long gone.

Globalism and nationalism have irreconcilable ends. Globalism is undermining our sense of national identity, our connection to the government. The American economy was placed in the hands of globalists—*all* recent administrations have promoted and said starry-eyed things about the magic of the global economy—and now the economy is like a plate being balanced on a stick by a circus clown. There's a lot of funny money out there spinning around, and any number of factors could send us further into financial decline. We're dependent on cheap imported technology, cheap imported food, cheap imported fuel. A dramatic spike in gas prices or a major national disaster could easily turn a volatile place like Southern California into a war zone. States are selling their own toll highways to foreign nations for short-term cash infusions. There's already a sense among people under forty that the money they pay into Social Security won't be there—or won't be worth anything—by the time they get old. People who work know they are throwing money into a black hole. Others are working the system and taking whatever they can get. Without endless economic growth, the United States won't be able to make good on its promises of endless prosperity and security. As things get worse and the State seems powerless to help, the State will seem less and less legitimate. People will lose their moral connection to it. Laws will seem more like revenue traps and shakedowns. The State will start to seem more like another extortion racket, and, as in Mexico, people will have a harder time telling the good guys from the bad guys. The U.S. of *us* will become the U.S. of *them*, and we'll Balkanize from within. If not officially, then unofficially. It's already happening.

The new Way of Women depends on prosperity, security, and globalism.

Any return of honor and The Way of Men and the eventual restoration of balance and harmony between the sexes will require the weakening of all three.

One of my favorite books is Anthony Burgess' *The Wanting Seed*. It's a sci-fi novel that tells the story of a future when, due to overpopulation, the State encourages homosexuality and effeminacy and officially discourages reproductive families. Throughout the book, Burgess writes about a theory of cyclical history that moves through three phases: *Pelphase*, *Interphase*, and *Gusphase*. In the Gusphase, named after St. Augustine, humanity is viewed through the eyes of a stern father who expects men to be violent and untrustworthy. Men see only what Peterson and Wrangham would call the "demonic" in each other, and those who seek order rule with an iron fist. After a period of security, people demonstrate that they can behave reasonably well, and men start to think that people are not so bad after all. Thinking shifts into the Pelphase mode, named for St. Pelagius, wherein men see each other as intrinsically good, peaceful, and perfectible through the gentle, guiding touch of social reform. However, this rose-colored, "noble savage" view of man does not reflect his nature, either. Man can't always be trusted to always follow the rules. He plays the system and does what he wants, and that leads to distrust, disorder, and disillusionment. This is when, as Burgess put it:

"Disappointment opens up a vista of chaos."[77]

During the middle phase of the cycle, called Interphase, there is violence and chaos and tyranny. It's a great shake-up that brings about another Gusphase, and eventually, a new Pelphase, and the cycle continues.

Men will not reassert themselves in any meaningful way through additional tweaking of an optimistic Pelagian system that is based on a pleasant denial of human nature. Men will reassert their interests during the Interphase. When states weaken and become "hollow" as futurist John Robb[78] believes they will, men will assert their interests through a return to their most basic social form. When the aching womb of the state can no longer provide the services or the security that keep men passive and dependent, localized groups of men who trust each other will build smaller networks to protect and further their own interests. In the presence of weak tyranny and the absence of strong nationalism, the shepherds will gather round their Robin Hoods, and they will found new tribes.

In the chaos that follows disappointment, gangs of men can restart the world.

Their future—the one world nanny state from cradle to grave, the global civilization of managers and clerks, the thin consumer identities, the bonobo masturbation society—is already showing signs of stress. Their future is based on unsustainable illusions and lies about human nature. Their future requires too many men to deny their own immediate interests to serve an abstract "greater good" that is far beyond human scale. All over the world, the *Star Trek* future that was once considered "inevitable" is starting to look improbable. The European Union is struggling, the global economy is faltering, and every day more people are starting to acknowledge that America is in a decline from which it will not recover.

Their future is already falling. It just needs a push.

If you want to push things toward The Way of Men and start the Interphase, create disappointment.

Throughout 2011, "Occupy Wall Street" protesters camped out in public parks across the country. They were angry about something. They weren't sure what. Their messages were incoherent. They were desperate. They wanted the government to come to their rescue. They wanted the government to fix things. They wanted the government to stop "corporate greed" as if it is possible to demand that global corporations stop acting to maximize profit. The "occupants" still just barely believed the dream that the State is beholden to the will of the people. They still wanted to believe that the State cares what they want. They wanted to believe that the State wants them to be happy. They were emotionally attached to the idea that the government cares, but they already suspected that it doesn't.

It doesn't, because it can't. Like global corporations, States have escaped human scale. There is no "man" to fight. States are institutions whose ultimate goals are survival, perpetuation, and expansion.

When the protesters went home, they achieved nothing. Nothing changed, though a few talking heads offered reassurances that the protesters had been heard.

People need to stop looking to the State for help and direction. They must become disillusioned and disappointed. To push things in a direction that is ultimately—though not immediately—better for men, the emotional connection between the people and the State must be severed completely. When the body of the people is released from the head of the sovereign, chaos will ensue. In that chaos, men will find themselves. They will stop looking to the State for help and start looking to each other. Together, men can create smaller, tighter, more localized systems.

People say they want a world that's more rational, but a world that's out of step with human nature isn't more rational at all.

Men aren't getting more rational.

They're getting weaker.

They're getting more fearful.

They're giving up more and more control.

There is no high road.

The only way out for men is The Way of the Gang.

"Only where the state ends, there begins the human being who is not superfluous: there begins the song of necessity, the unique and inimitable tune."

—Friedrich Nietzche, *Thus Spake Zarathustra*

HOW TO START A GANG

Any return to The Way of Men is probably going to happen in hollow states through extra-legal means. Gangs form out of necessity, or to exploit opportunities. Gangs are going to gain the most traction in areas where State influence is weak, creating both necessity and opportunity. Furthermore, gangs are proto-states. Proto-states threaten the power of larger existing states, so when men form proto-states to assert their own interests, their actions will be outlawed by those states.

It is not my intent here to tell you how to start a criminal enterprise.

I have romanticized gangs somewhat to make a point about the nature of men, but I am not suffering from any delusion that modern gangs are run by "good guys" who take from the rich and give to the poor. I have every reason to believe that life in a gang today would be nasty, brutish, and short. I have every reason to believe that life in a gang existing inside a collapsed State would be nasty, brutish, and short. There is no shortage of evidence about gang brutality, infighting, human trafficking, rape, or murder almost for the sake of murder alone. Wrangham and Peterson called the gang impulse male "demonism" for some good reasons.

The conclusion I reached while writing this book was that the gang is the kernel of masculine identity. I believe it is also the kernel of ethnic, tribal, and national identity. The culture of the gang is, as author bell hooks wrote in a rather different context, "the essence of patriarchal masculinity."[79]

If you want to follow The Way of Men, if you want to advance a return to honor and manly virtue, if you want to steel yourself against an uncertain future—start a gang.

Honor requires an honor group, a group of men with similar values. Honor requires the possibility of dishonor in the eyes of peers whose respect you value. The cultivation of manly virtue is accelerated by completion and the expectations of male peers. And, if you want to become resilient to uncertainty and chaos, you need a circle of men who you trust and who you can depend on.

Some readers will inevitably respond: "My wife/girlfriend is awesome. She takes boxing and shoots guns and fixes cars. She's my partner."

That's nice. But if your strategy for the future is holing up with ma and the chillins, your strategy sucks. I don't care if your girlfriend is a Certified Ninja, she's not worth eight men. *Kill Bill* was not a documentary. A strong and skillful woman will be worth more to you in a crisis than a prima donna, but she can't replace men in your life. No woman can take the place of men in a man's life.

It is evolutionarily sound for women to want to secure your commitment to them and attempt to place themselves at the center of your world. They'll want to be involved in everything you do, and they'll be on guard against perceived threats to their security and your commitment.

Men have been negotiating the "crisis of masculinity"—the push and pull between civilized domesticity and lure of gang life—for centuries. Men need to set boundaries and make time for men in their lives. It's important to their sense of identity, it's important to their sense of security and belonging, and it's good survival strategy. Part of the reason we are where we are right now is that men stopped depending on each other and started depending on the State. The family unit is not enough. A support network of ten is better than a support network of two.

To get a sense of how one might go about expanding that support network and "start a gang," here's a working definition of what a gang really is, based on the idea of men bonding, creating a group identity, and setting up a perimeter:

Gang - A bonded, hierarchical coalition of males allied to assert their interests against external forces.

A gang is essentially a male group identity; it's an *us*. It's a go-to group of men allied against *them*.

In an emergency situation, the *us* is often defined by proximity. You've seen the movie. A bunch of unlikely characters get stuck together by unforeseen circumstances and are forced to work out their differences and learn to depend on each other. That could certainly happen, but depending on the luck of the draw isn't a great strategy. Picking your team is a better strategy.

Create Proximity

The Internet is a good filter. It's a good way to find men who share some of your values. However, your friends on message boards and on social networking sites, scattered all over the world, are not going to be there for you when the proverbial shit hits the fan. Spend more time making contact with men who are geographically close to you. If you have close friends in your area, consider moving into the same apartment complex or within a few blocks of one another. Think about the way gangs start in inner cities. Men and boys have lived and died to defend tribes with territories as small as a few blocks. Proximity creates familiarity and shared identity. It creates *us*. Spreading our alliances across nations and continents keeps us reliant on the power of the State and the global economy. Men who are separated and have no one else to rely on must rely on the State.

Choose Your Us

A lot of factors could define the boundaries of *us* against *them*. If your religion is important to you, that's a good place to start. Mormon men, for instance, would probably fall into a community gang fairly easily. If your ethnic heritage or race is something you feel strongly about, as is very often the case with gangs, then that might be your starting point. Familiarity and likeness make trust easier to establish. However, sports teams make out well enough with men from very different backgrounds. If a desirable superordinate goal—like survival—is introduced, it has been proven that men can put aside all sorts of differences.

Men with opposing viewpoints can respect each other and enjoy civilized debates, but when it comes to forming *us*, it's better to have a group of men who are on the same page about the issues most important to them.

If you have decided after reading this book that you want to return to The Way of Men, the men in your gang will have to be committed to undermining the globalist masturbation society, hollowing out the State, and reviving a culture of honor.

Create Fraternity

A gang is a fraternity, a bonded brotherhood of men. That

said; don't start trying to figure out your colors or your secret handshake just yet. These kinds of male cultural phenomena will occur organically as the result of shared history and identity. Only huge organizations like the Army can effectively sort a bunch of men into a group and artificially create a gang or brotherhood. It is possible for political movements to do this, but if they appear to be openly anti-government, their high profile is going to attract the attention of the authorities.

You don't need a formal group or a membership charter, and you don't need to elect a president. What you need is face time. You can bond with men online, but only to a point. People can hide online in ways that they can't in person. Men are tactical thinkers. They guard themselves. To get to know a man you need to spend time with him, you need to do things together, you need to build trust. Don't expect a casual acquaintance to have your back when you're in trouble. A solid friendship is just like any other relationship. It requires give and take. It requires some time and some history.

If you know some guys you can connect with, and who are on more or less the same page philosophically, make sure you make time for them. Set aside time to create that history and build that trust. Even women who are "like one of the guys" will have a chilling effect on that process. Men are not honest with each other in the same way when women are present, and establishing trust requires honesty. Men are going to want to have girlfriends and wives and families and other connections with women in their lives, and that is all well and good, but as I said, you can't expect men who don't really know you to help you through tough times. Put in the effort. Eating and drinking together is fine, but it makes more sense to plan tactically oriented outings. You need to learn how to read each other and work together as a group. Go to the shooting range. Go hunting. Play paintball. Go to the gym. Take martial arts classes. Join a sports team. Take a workshop. Learn a useful skill. Fix something. Build something.

Make something. Get off your asses and *do* something.

In harder times, the men that you do these kinds of things with are going to be the first men you call. They will be your gang. They will be your us.

I'm going to close this book with some Viking wisdom concerning male friendship from *The Sayings of Hár*, also known as the *Hávamál*.

If friend thou hast whom faithful thou deemest,

And wishest to win him for thee:

Open thy heart to him nor withhold thy gifts,

And fare to find him often.

If faithful friend thou hast found for thee,

Then fare thou find him full oft;

Overgrown is soon with tall grass and bush

The trail which is trod by no one.[80]

ENDNOTES

1   Some studies have shown a major decrease in male testosterone over the last 20 years (see below). That drop may be due to something in the water but it's likely a result of widespread obesity. I'd bet it also has something to with a relative loss of social status and the proliferation of safe, sedentary lifestyles. If testosterone really has dropped in a few decades, it proves that men and women were more different in the past and that future studies claiming similarities between the sexes will be less relevant when looking at historical ideas about sex differences.

Travison, Thomas G., Andre B. Araujo, Amy B. O'Donnell, Varant Kupelian, and John B. McKinlay. "A Population-Level Decline in Serum Testosterone Levels in American Men." *The Journal of Clinical Endocrinology & Metabolism* 92.11 Jan. (2007): 196-202. Web. 5 Dec. 2011.

2   Junger, Sebastian. WAR. Hachette Book Group, 2010. 242. Print.
3   W. -X. Zhou, D. Sornette, R. A. Hill and R. I. M. Dunbar. "Discrete Hierarchical Organization of Social Group Sizes" *Proceedings: Biological Sciences*, Vol. 272, No. 1561 (Feb. 22, 2005), pp. 439-444.

Also: Search "Dunbar's Number" or review articles about scientist Robin Dunbar.

4   McDonnell, Myles. *Roman Manliness : Virtus and the Roman Republic.* Cambridge University Press, 2006. 4. Print.

5   ADDITIONAL NOTE (2021 Edition). This concept is developed substantially in my 2021 book, *Fire in the Dark*. Vir is not merely the Latin word for "man;" the root is actually much older. The Latin comes from the Proto-Italic

178   *The Way of Men*

*wiros, from Proto-Indo-European *wiHrós. This is related to the Sanskrit "vīrá",, the Old Norse "verr" and the Old English "wer," which readers may recognize as part of the modern word "wer(e)wolf" -- meaning both man and wolf. In the majority of these very different cultures, the "vir"-related word for "man" may also imply "hunter," "warrior," or "hero." It has been theorized that the Proto-Indo-European word root *wiHrós was derived from the word in the same theoretical language that meant "to hunt."

6   It is also true that manhood, by necessity, becomes increasingly metaphorical with age. An older man who can no longer compete with other men or hunt and fight will focus on developing other virtues.

7   Chee, Rosie. "Breaking the Myth: Increasing Testosterone In Females = Muscle Accretion, Strength Gains, And Fat Loss." *Bodybuilding.com*. 15 Oct. 2009. Web. 11 July 2011. http://www.bodybuilding.com/fun/myth-of-women-lifting-heavy2.htm

8   I use these terms interchangeably, as I believe average people do. There is an orthodoxy in academia that prefers to make a distinction between masculinity and manliness, and this distinction serves the ideology of feminists and cultural determinists. For more on this debate, Harvey C. Mansfield outlined his reasons for writing about manliness instead of masculinity in his 2006 book, *Manliness.*

9   Maffly, Brian. "U. biologist argues humans stood up to fight, not walk." *Salt Lake Tribune* 18 May 2011. Web. 11 July 2011

10   *The Nichomachean Ethics*. Trans. David Ross. Oxford World's Classics ed. N.p.: Oxford University Press, 1998. 63-73. Print.

11   It is from the Latin word virtus that we get the English word "virtue." This is due to the expansion of the concept of virtus in the later stages of the Roman Empire, where it absorbed a wider range of other values and became a kind of "moralized masculinity." McDonnell's thesis was that this was not always so, and he provided numerous examples from early Roman literature and records to prove that the early Romans equated virtus ("manliness") with martial valor.

12   McDonnell, Myles. *Roman Manliness : Virtus and the Roman Republic*. Cambridge University Press, 2006. 4. Print.

13   Ibid. 12.

14   Ibid. 31.

15   *Livy. The Rise of Rome: Books One to Five* (Bks. 1-5) Book 2: 12. (Kindle Locations 1482-1484). Kindle.

16   Ibid.

17   *Republic*. Trans. Allan Bloom. Basic Books, 1968. 89. Print. (Book 3: 410d-e)

18   Also transliterated "thymos." θύμος.

19   *Republic*. Trans. Allan Bloom. Basic Books, 1968. 449. Print. (Notes, Book 2: 33)

20   *Republic*. Trans. Allan Bloom. Basic Books, 1968. 52. Print. (Book 2: 373-376)

21   Kruger, Daniel J. "Sexual selection and the Male:Female Mortality Ratio." *Evolutionary Psychology 2* (2004): 66-85. Web. 11 Aug. 2011.

22   Sheridan, Sam. *A Fighter's Heart : One Man's Journey Through the World of Fighting*. Grove Press, 2007. 280. Print.

23   This is a common topic in the "manosphere" and the "game" community. I do not believe that alphas and betas are fixed types. I use these labels (as I have above) to describe dominant and submissive relationships between given sets of men. A man can be near the top of one hierarchy and near the bottom in another. One man's alpha can be another man's beta. This makes sense in our primate-based gang model, where members test each other and change roles. Even insular hierarchies shift, and the male on top today may not be in charge tomorrow.

24   Hobbes, Thomas. *Leviathan*. 1651. Cambridge University Press, 1996. 65. Print.

25   Bowman, James. *Honor : A History*. Encounter Books, 2006. 6. Print.

26   Collin D. Barnes, Ryan Brown, and Michael Tamborski. "Living Dangerously: Culture of Honor, Risk-Taking, and the Nonrandomness of "Accidental" Deaths." Social Psychological and Personality Science. June 8, 2011 1948550611410440, first published on June 8, 2011. Online.

http://spp.sagepub.com/content/early/2011/06/03/1948550611410440

27   Carollo, Kim. ""Honor Culture" Linked to Accidental Deaths." http://abcnews.go.com. ABC, 15 Aug. 2011. Web. 28 Aug. 2011.

http://abcnews.go.com/Health/honor-culture-linked-higher-rate-accidental-deaths-south/story?id=14292632

28   Barnes et al.

29   Bowman, James. *Honor : A History*. Encounter Books, 2006. 38. Print.

30   Hamilton died from a wound suffered in a pistol duel with Vice President Aaron Burr in 1804.

31   Michael, Kimmel S. "Masculinity as Homophobia." *Reconstructing Gender : A Multicultural Anthology*. Ed. Estelle Disch. 3rd ed. McGraw Hill, 2003. 103-09. Web. 8 Sept. 2011.

32   Schnarch, Brian. "Neither Man nor Woman: Berdache — A Case for Non-Dichotomous Gender Construction." *Anthropologica* 34.1 (1992): 105-21. JSTOR. Web. 8 Sept. 2011.

33   The author's favorite (Godfathers I & II exempted), is a British gangster flick: *The Long Good Friday* (1980)

34   Newell, Waller R., ed. *What is a Man? 3,000 Years of Wisdom on the Art of Manly Virtue*. ReganBooks/HarperCollins, 2000. Print.

35   Ibid. XVIII.

36   "About Us." The Art of Manliness. Ed. Brett McKay. N.p., n.d. Web. 14 June 2011. http://artofmanliness.com/about-2

37   McKay, Brett. Message to the author. 30 June 2011. E-mail.

38   For more on this, read my short book *No Man's Land*, available online at:

https://www.jack-donovan.com/sowilo/2018/08/08/no-mans-land/

39   Connell, Robert William. *Masculinities*. University of California Press, 1995. 67-86. Print.

40   Ibid. 69.

41   ADDITIONAL NOTE (2021 Edition). Over the years, the phrase "There is a difference between being a good man and being good at being a man" has proved a major takeaway from *The Way of Men*. It was only during an exchange with *Sovereignty* author Ryan Michler many years after the original 2012 publication of the book that I realized that I had subconsciously borrowed that phrasing from a book I had read in 2006 while doing research for a much earlier project. The phrase is quoted in David Gilmore's *Manhood in the Making* (Yale University, 1990.), from anthropologist Michael Herzfeld's *The Poetics of Manhood: Contest and Identity in a Cretan Mountain Village* (Princeton University Press, 1985.) I vaguely remember reading parts of Herzfeld's work in addition to Gilmore's book early in my study of academic work concerning men and masculinity. While I didn't even realize that I had done it, I lifted the phrasing Herzfeld had used when writing about a small, somewhat isolated culture and applied it very broadly to make an important distinction and solve a persistent problem that men tend to have when they discuss masculinity. It is almost impossible to have a coherent discussion about universal aspects of masculinity unless you separate them from discussions about morality — because morality is always relative to a particular group, not only in terms of religion or culture, but in terms of the relation of one group to another group. This distinction between morality and masculinity is one of the things that made *The Way of Men* such an important and clarifying book for so many men, and that is different in intent and influence from what Herzfeld was doing in his anthropological study. But since I became aware of it, I wanted to give credit where it is due in this updated edition.

42   Dickie, John. *Cosa Nostra : A History of the Sicilian Mafia*. 2004. 31. Palgrave McMillan, 2005. Print.

43   Kaplan, David E., and Alec Dubro. Yakuza : Japan's Criminal Underworld. University of California Press, 2003. 17. Print.

44   Isikoff, Michael. "Feds Crack Down on 'Robin Hood' Drug Cartel." The Daily Beast (Newsweek). N.p., 22 Oct. 2009. Web. 4 Oct. 2011. https://www.newsweek.com/feds-crack-down-robin-hood-drug-cartel-216820

45   Gibbs, Stephen. "'Family values' of Mexico drug gang." BBC News. BBC, 22 Oct. 2009. Web. 4 Oct. 2011. http://news.bbc.co.uk/2/hi/8319924.stm

46   "Message of the Secretary-General for 2011." International Day for the Elimination of Violence against Women 25 November. Ed. Ban Ki-moon. The United Nations, 25 Nov. 2011. Web. 9 Jan. 2012.

http://www.un.org/en/events/endviolenceday/sgmessages.shtml

47   Margaret, Mead. *Sex and Temperament: In Three Primitive Societies*. 1935. Harper Perennial, 2001. 262. Print.

48   For more on "Reimagining Masculinity," see No Man's Land, available online at:

https://www.jack-donovan.com/sowilo/2018/08/08/no-mans-land/

49   Livius, Titus. *The Rise of Rome*. Oxford's World Classics.

50   Wrangham, Richard, and Dale Peterson. *Demonic Males : Apes and the Origins of Human Violence*. New York: Mariner Books/Houghton Mifflin Company, 1996. 248. Print.

51   James, William. "The Moral Equivalent of War." Wikisource. Originally published 1906. Web. 15 Sept. 2011. http://en.wikisource.org/wiki/The_Moral_Equivalent_of_War

52   Darwin, Charles. *The Descent of Man*. Orig. 1871. New Century Books. Kindle. Loc. 2623-2624.

53   Goldman, David P. (aka. "Spengler") "The fifth horseman of the apocalypse." *Asia Times Online* 13 Dec. 2011. Web. 6 Feb. 2012.

54   *28 Days Later*. Writ. Alex Garland. 2002. 20th Century Fox. DVD-ROM.

55   Keeley, Lawrence H. *War Before Civilization*. Oxford University Press, 1996. 1,016-172. Kindle.

56   de Waal, Frans. *Chimpanzee Politics*. 1982. Baltimore: Johns Hopkins Paperbacks, 2000. 1,055-58. Kindle.

57   Wrangham, Richard, and Dale Peterson. 205.

58   Keen, Sam. *Fire in the Belly*. Bantam, 1991. Chapter 8, "A Brief History of Manhood." Print. 1,655-2,110. Kindle.

59   Brown, Donald E. "Human Universals." DePaul University, n.d. Web. 19 Feb. 2011. http://condor.depaul.edu/mfiddler/hyphen/humunivers.htm

60   Wolf, Naomi. "The Porn Myth." *New York Magazine*. 20 Oct. 2003. Web. 18 Sept. 2011. http://nymag.com/nymetro/news/trends/n_9437/

61   Amsden, David. "Not Tonight, Honey. I'm Logging On." *New York Magazine*. 20 Oct. 2003. Web. 18 Sept. 2011. http://nymag.com/nymetro/news/trends/n_9349/

62   Rothbart, Davy. "He's Just Not That Into Anyone." *New York Magazine*. 30 Jan. 2011. Web. 18 Sept. 2011. http://nymag.com/news/features/70976/

63   Friedan, Betty. *The Feminine Mystique*. 1963. Dell Publishing, 1983. 15. Print.

64   Matthew, Crawford B. *Shop Class As Soulcraft : an inquiry into the value of*

work. Penguin Books, 2010. 44. Print.

65   Glaze, Lauren. "NCJ 231681 : Correctional Populations In The United States, 2009." Office of Justice Programs. Bureau of Justice Statistics, 21 Dec. 2010. Web. 2 Oct. 2011.

http://bjs.ojp.usdoj.gov/index.cfm?ty=pbdetail&iid=2316

According to the document cited, in 2009 there were 3,911,300 men under "community supervision either on probation or parole" and 2,086,400 men "held in the custody of state or federal prisons or local jails." The total of both groups was 5,997,700 men. There were about 1,241,625 men on active duty in the armed forces during the same year.

66   *The Epic of Gilgamesh*. Trans. N. K. Sanders. Penguin Classics, ePenguin, 1973. 61-72. Print. Loc 944-1091. Kindle.

67   Hobbes, Thomas. *Leviathan*. 1651. Cambridge University Press, 1996. 42. Print.

68   *The Epic of Gilgamesh*. Trans. N. K. Sanders. Penguin Classics, ePenguin, 1973. 102. Print. Loc 1483. Kindle.

69   Tiger, Lionel. *The Decline of Males*. 1999. Golden Books. Print. 257.

70   Garcia, Guy (2008-10-07). *The Decline of Men* (p. 268). HarperCollins e-books. Kindle Edition.

71   Wilson, James Q. "Burying the Hatchet." *The Wall Street Journal* 1 Oct. 2011. Web. 4 Oct. 2011. http://online.wsj.com/article/SB100014240531119043 32804576537813826824914.html

72   Chomsky, Noam. *Understanding Power: The Indispensable Chomsky*. The New York Press, 2002. 88-89. Print.

73   "Drug violence mars Mexico city." BBC News. Ed. Stephanie Gibbs. BBC News, Cancun, 19 Feb. 2009. Web. 4 Oct. 2011. http://news.bbc.co.uk/2/hi/americas/7897345.stm

74   Harrigan, Steve. "America's Third War: As Drug Cartels Continue Stronghold, Female Mexican Police Chief Taken Near Christmas Still Missing." FoxNews.com. Ed. Steve Harrigan. 8 Feb. 2011. Web. 4 Oct. 2011. http://www.foxnews.com/us/2011/02/08/americas-war-female-mexican-chief-police-missing-christmas

75   "Tijuana violence slows as one cartel takes control." http://www.reuters.com. Ed. Lizbeth Diaz. *Reuters*, 5 Sept. 2011. Web. 4 Oct. 2011. http://www.reuters.com/article/2011/09/05/us-mexico-drugs-tijuana-idUSTRE7844EX20110905

76   Schwirtz, Michael. "Vory v Zakone has hallowed place in Russian criminal lore." *New York Times*. N.p., 29 July 2008. Web. 4 Oct. 2011. http://www.nytimes.com/2008/07/29/world/europe/29iht-moscow.4.14865004.html

77   Burgess, Anthony. *The Wanting Seed*. W.W. Norton & Co., 1962. 19. Print.

78   See Robb's http://globalguerrillas.typepad.com/globalguerrillas/ site

for articles and up-to-the-minute thinking about "hollow states" and creating "resilient communities."

79   hooks, bell (2007-03-16). *We Real Cool* (p. 26). Taylor & Francis. Kindle Edition.

80   *The Poetic Edda*. Trans. Lee M. Hollander. 2nd ed. University of Texas Press, 1962. 21, 32. Print. (The archaic "Ope" in the Hollander was updated in this text to "open" for clarity.)

SUPPLEMENTARY MATERIAL

AFTERWORD - 2022

I chose to make my commentary on the tenth-anniversary edition of this book an Afterword because I didn't want to muddy up the first pages of the book with an introduction.

The Way of Men begins exactly as it should — simply, humbly, and honestly.

The Greeks would have invoked the muses, but *The Way of Men* was written by a delivery truck driver making $12.50 an hour.

I won't try to convince you that I've ever been exactly "normal" or "average," or that I was somehow burdened by poverty or misfortune — but that's what I was doing at the time.

As I went back over this text to prepare this edition, I was impressed by that delivery truck driver's effort and his attention to detail. (There are a lot more footnotes than I remembered.) I was also struck by how much I still believe what he wrote. I stand by *The Way of Men* and believe it is the most important book I will ever write.

I will probably never father a son of my own, but it is through *The Way of Men* that, in some small way, I became a kind of father figure to many. I wrote the words that their fathers couldn't or wouldn't say, or I explained things more clearly than their fathers were able to explain them. One of the most humbling experiences for me has been reading emails and messages from men telling me that they've bought a copy of *The Way of Men* to give to their sons. Some of the men I've influenced have had little or no contact with their fathers at all. I'm proud that I was able to help them in some way.

That guy carrying boxes of potatoes into restaurant kitchens while it was still dark outside had no idea that his little black book would go on to sell hundreds of thousands of copies or be translated into Polish, Portuguese, French, Spanish, German, and Italian. But I think *The Way of Men* connected with so many men precisely because it was that guy who wrote it.

The Way of Men wasn't some sterile and theoretical pontification issued from the cloistered confines of a university library. It was written at night and on days off by a guy who spent some time in college but whose real education came from working for the better part of two decades in all kinds of professional offices and warehouses and restaurants. I wasn't a journalist or a pundit or a professional talking head. I wasn't raised poor, but there was no silver spoon or golden trust fund parachute. I'm glad that I had to make my own way in the world.

When I wrote *The Way of Men*, I was a man in my late thirties who had done a lot of different kinds of work and moved through many different groups of men. I'd been out shooting guns in the woods with rednecks, and I'd been out partying in the big city.

I found myself moving through many worlds of men, but I wasn't exactly "of" any of them. I was a fellow traveler, and I shared joy and work and suffering with men, but I was always a little bit of an outsider, always observing. I could afford to take a one thousand foot view because I owed no particular group my allegiance.

I grew up beside a cornfield in rural Pennsylvania in the 1980s, where I dreamed the cliche dream of moving to the big city in New York to become a "somebody." And when I did move to New York City in the early 1990s, I wanted to go everywhere and see everything. At seventeen years old, I walked all over that city. I went to see operas, and I went to museums and galleries. I've always been interested in sex and gender. Back then, I would have considered myself some kind of feminist. I went to see controversial author Camille Paglia read from her latest book of essays. She signed a copy of *Vamps & Tramps* that I lost decades ago. I went to a design school affiliated with the New School for Social Research, where I hung out with all kinds of coked-up socialists and progressives. I worked in nightclubs and interned for an East Village fashion designer when I wasn't in school. I was surrounded by transgressive art and subversive narratives about sex, gender, and social organization.

It all seemed new and exciting and different. I believed in many of the ideas and causes that these writers and artists were advancing. It is possible that, had I stayed in the isolated social bubbles of the New York art and design worlds, I would be playing for an entirely different team right now and saying altogether different things.

The gods, however, had other plans for me...

I ended up moving around and doing all kinds of jobs, and I learned — usually the hard way — how the world actually worked from a number of different perspectives. I learned that there were differences between what people say and what they do, and between how they'd like to be seen and how they actually behave. I saw it in the patrons of the New York City nightclubs that I worked in — where I frequently came in contact with celebrities before I was even old enough to drink legally. And I saw it years later in the working-class people and their managers at so many low-paying jobs. I saw it in the cubicles and offices when working for big corporations. I wouldn't say that this made me cynical, but I would say that it made me realistic. Working and living — real life — changed my mind about a lot of things.

I watched how high-minded policies created by the bureaucrats and academics who went to schools like the one I went to play out "on the ground" for most men. I watched — and felt — how crassly the interests and complaints of average and middle-class men were dismissed.

When you read the last few chapters of *The Way of Men*, you can tell that they were written by a guy who had been shuffled through employment and government agencies. A guy who had been tested and drug screened and treated like a sub-human resource, who had been forced to watch and "sign off" on countless smug, condescending videos on job safety and diversity and sexual harassment and corporate policy. You can feel my very real anger and frustration in those pages.

While there are timeless concepts in *The Way of Men* that could be presented without those rants, I think the rawness of those tirades contributed to the book's success and the emotional connection that many men have to it.

A lot of the men who read the book are going through the same shit right now that I was going through then. It's been a decade, and I know that what they are going through now is even worse — so my experiences and frustrations have remained fresh and relevant.

As an older man with a much larger audience, I would probably turn the anger in my rhetoric down a bit and take a more careful and measured approach. My focus now would shift more toward the creation of order and less on anger and destruction. You can see that in my latest book, *Fire in the Dark*. Still, the creation of order is very often preceded by thumotic anger and destruction, so there is something very natural about this progression of thought.

As an older man who has accomplished more, who would love to keep doing what he's doing — as a man with more skin in the game — I really don't want to see humanity "go into a Dark Age for a few hundred years and think about what it's done." I think we should all be wary of the unintended consequences of innovation, but I'm no Luddite. I love new technology and the opportunities it creates for new forms of creation, culture, and art.

However, I also don't want to die in slavery or see men progressively emasculated, chemically neutered, and controlled.

Sniping critics have dreamed up all kinds of insulting reasons why I might have become an advocate for men and masculinity and why I might have written *The Way of Men*. The truth is that I recognized that something noble in the world was being actively destroyed and replaced with something that was far less admirable.

I recognized that heroic masculinity — or put even more simply, masculinity — was and is being replaced by mediocrity and servility. What I later called "The First Men" — the men who create and defend order, the men around the fire, the men who protect The Perimeter — those men are being replaced by what Nietzsche would have called "The Last Men."

I never refer to myself as a warrior. Warriors make war, and the word is cheapened when it is applied to everyone who pushes through a workout or gets over a bad day. Many have suggested otherwise, but I don't have a fantasy about how "cool" war would be or imagine that I'd be some magnificent Achilles. I hope I never have to make war, but it is the thumotic, heroic aspect of me that made me want to devote my life to fighting — however metaphorically or intellectually — to preserve and reinvigorate the heroic spirit in man.

I've somehow managed to make a living doing this, but there are much easier ways to make money. It's never been about that. At the moment, I make about as much as an average middle manager or a successful tattoo artist. I've sacrificed a lot of opportunities, and I'll certainly never be welcome in certain portions of "polite society." But I've also met men whom I admire — men who are better at being men and better men than I am — whom I would never have met otherwise. I've been invited into circles I never would have dreamed I'd be invited into.

Advocating for men and masculinity has become my life's work, and I wouldn't trade it for anything. Someone had to do it, and I felt called to the work, even though I was and am an unlikely candidate at best. But, being an unlikely candidate gave me an edge.

Most books written about masculinity are prescriptive. They are written from a particular moral perspective and aim to encourage a target group of men to behave in a particular way. This is true of every feminist book about masculinity, but it is also true of almost every conservative book about masculinity. The message is never just "be a man," it is always "be a man like me" or "be a man who does what I want men to do."

When I was a young man, I hated the kinds of men who always made masculinity about themselves and whatever they liked to do and whatever they believed. It's one of the reasons why I used to think masculinity was stupid and called myself a feminist. Those guys are always mocking and emasculating men who aren't exactly like them. I can hear Mick Jagger singing the line, "but he can't be a man 'cause he doesn't smoke the same cigarettes as me." That's how a lot of men are, unfortunately. A man has to drink whiskey, or he has to care about working on cars, or he has to watch football. These are all superficial cultural associations with masculinity that change as you move from one group of men to another.

The same is true when it comes to many moral associations with masculinity. Christian authors insist that "real men" behave the way that their given denomination says that men should behave, but a very large percentage of men in the world today are not members of that particular denomination. Are those other men not "real" men? Are they not authentically masculine?

It was too easy for me to see how these cultural and moral details and associations were specific to groups and therefore couldn't be essential parts of any discussion about masculinity as a universal experience or phenomenon.

Separating masculinity from morality, as I did in the chapter "On Being A Good Man," is one of the most important contributions that I think *The Way of Men* made to the broader discussion about masculinity as a concept. That resonated with a lot of men and stuck with them, and I've had it repeated back to me over and over.

The Way of Men wasn't written for one group of men, or for my group of men. *The Way of Men* was written for all men. *The Way of Men* was my attempt to determine what masculinity is, what men from different groups have in common, how men have always behaved, and why. *The Way of Men* was meant to be — and I believe that it is and has been — revelatory. The basic ideas about masculinity discussed in this book apply to cops and criminals and Christians and pagans and Muslims. They apply to blacks, whites, Asians, and everyone else.

That's the reason I put skeletons on the original cover instead of Vikings or knights or samurai. Skulls may seem like a dark or morbid choice, but everyone can relate to them. Every man can recognize something about himself in a skull — it doesn't matter what race he is or what faith he professes.

One recurring criticism of *The Way of Men* is that it presents value in both individual liberty and group loyalty, which requires a sacrifice of individual liberty. Some misunderstand this as a contradiction or inconsistency. I prefer to consider it a paradox.

If you attempt to resolve a paradox by shifting all the way in either direction, you'll inevitably just make things worse for everyone.

"If we just went all the way in this one direction, everything would be better" is a foolish young man's argument — or the echoed argument of a man who is trying to exploit him.

You can't "solve" a paradox. The best you can do is seek the best balance, and like any balancing act, you have to keep adjusting to stay balanced. America's Founding Fathers struggled with the same paradox. The Continental Army was fighting for increased individual liberty, but in order to do that, men had to be willing to enlist in an army with rules and strict discipline. The Founders wanted to create a free nation, or at least a nation that valued liberty more than the nation they fought to break away from. But even a free country requires some law and order.

In fact, law and order are required on some level to protect individual liberty. If you don't respect individual liberty enough, you end up with dystopian tyranny. If you don't respect order enough, you end up with dystopian chaos and anarchy.

The Way of Men addresses a related paradox in the chapter titled "A Check to Civilization" and again in the chapter "What is Best in Life?." Men have always worried about how much civilization was too much, just as they have always wondered how much of your independence you should sacrifice to belong to a group. There are good arguments for both directions in both cases. A workable resolution will always require some tenuous, balancing compromise that must be revisited continually and rebalanced as circumstances evolve.

People sometimes ask me if there's anything I would change about *The Way of Men*. I've received a handful of messages over the years telling me that I've "missed" one of the Tactical Virtues. However, those suggestions usually include some moral element and obviously come from someone who didn't get the whole "difference between being good at being a man and being a good man" thing. Guys have suggested "discipline" once or twice, but I think that is somewhat implied in the cultivation of virtues like Strength and Mastery. I've often thought that "Might" could make more sense than "Strength" because the Strength that men have to cultivate is too easily misunderstood as "powerlifting" strength. Primal masculinity is probably much more concerned with overall athleticism than putting the most weight on a bar, which is a fairly new concept -- though there has been a long history of competitive stone lifting among men. The word Strength still sounds better to my ear, and it would be a pointless change to make ten years after the fact.

While aspects of *The Way of Men* may have seemed extremist or alarmist in 2012, the book has proved to be eerily prophetic since the "pandemic" of 2020 and onward. Two members of the "skeleton gang" on the somewhat apocalyptic cover — included on the title page of this edition in stylized form — were even pictured wearing gaiters or "masks." The contrast between those who would trade freedom for the presumed "safety" of an existence completely controlled by central planners and those, like myself, who see that as a dystopian nightmare has become increasingly stark.

In 2012, the public conversation about masculinity was characterized by smug feminist triumphalism. Only a small and motley group of men who seemed like cranky malcontents seemed to be concerned with the future of men and masculinity. They were often called losers and were more or less told that "real men don't think (or talk, or write) about masculinity." Mainstream advocates for masculinity like Jordan B. Peterson were only beginning to appear. Realistic assessments of the sexual marketplace and necessary criticisms of both conservative and feminist views on the differences between the sexes and the relationship between them — advanced first by victims of divorce court injustice, pick-up artists, political fringe groups, and those interested in evolutionary psychology — were only beginning to gain the attention of other men. Now, an entire generation of young men have come of age with access to these ideas through social media, books, conferences, private chats, and forums.

Today, I find myself surrounded by former members of Special Operations teams, elite athletes, successful businessmen, *New York Times* best-selling authors, teachers, rogue psychologists, pastors, priests, public figures, and even a handful of politicians. Men from every level of society have found that they can no longer ignore the coordinated and fully institutionalized attack on men and masculinity. They're concerned, not only for themselves, but for their sons, and for the future. They're getting involved and they're speaking out, and it is a powerful and inspiring thing to behold.

The Way of Men shows no signs of becoming less relevant. I feel gifted and grateful that I was able to write the right book at the right time. *The Way of Men* has become a foundational text for this phenomenally important movement — the aim of which is nothing less than the preservation and perpetuation of that which is and has always been the best in men.

It is in this spirit that I am publishing this 10th Anniversary hardcover edition of *The Way of Men*.

When I designed the cover of the original paperback, my aim was to create a book that looked kind of "metal" — like a graphic novel. A book that a young man would feel "cool" reading on a bus or a train. The cover of this edition is purposefully minimal and straightforward. I hope it will find its way to the bookshelves and libraries of fathers and sons and masculine thinkers — to be passed down and referenced long after I am gone.

Start the World —

Jack Donovan
Salt Lake City, Utah.
January 26, 2022

ABOUT THIS EDITION

In this edition, I'm including two pieces that were originally in some way intended to be part of *The Way of Men*: the essay "Violence is Golden," and the three-part essay that I've released as a free e-book online, "No Man's Land."

Violence is Golden

The essay "Violence is Golden" is the most popular essay I've ever written. "Violence is Golden" wasn't intended to romanticize violence or promote violence — though it could easily be portrayed that way by an ideological opponent, or interpreted that way by a sloppy reader. "Violence is Golden" simply acknowledges the inescapable reality that violence is a factor that underlies all human social organization. It always has been, and it always will be.

One of the most important points the essay makes is that the threat of violence backs up every human law — even laws advocated by people who consider themselves peaceful. I believe that understanding this marks the boundary between thinking like a child and understanding reality as an adult.

People who won't allow themselves to acknowledge the primacy of violence in human relations and ALL governments "left, right, or other," have not graduated to grown-up thinking, and they belong at the "kiddies table."

Dealing with the harsh reality of violence is and has always been the job of men — it is what men do and have always done "out there" at the edge of the perimeter between darkness and light and chaos and order. To write and speak about masculinity honestly and intelligently, one has to be prepared to acknowledge and address the inextricable relationship between masculinity and violence.

"Violence is Golden" was originally written as the opening chapter of *The Way of Men*. The hardest part of writing is always the organization of ideas, and finding the most effective rhythm and flow for them. An idea can be truthful and even crucial, but it also has to be presented in the right way and at the right time.

I decided to start *The Way of Men* out differently, and published "Violence is Golden" on a long-defunct blog called *Arthur's Hall of Viking Manliness* in 2010. I met Arthur once. He really was a giant of a man, and he really did look like a Viking. He hosted a thriving forum for men at the time, and I remember going on a camping trip once with some of the members.

After "Violence is Golden" was initially published online, it was posted and re-posted and linked to across thousands of sites and forums frequented by firearms enthusiasts, as well as members of the military and law enforcement. I eventually posted it on my own site, and included it in a collection of essays I released, titled *A Sky Without Eagles*.

No Man's Land

The first draft of *The Way of Men* was much different from the version that was finally printed in 2012. It included a lot of the same material, but I was trying to do what other authors of mainstream books did at the time. That is, I was trying to acknowledge everyone else who was writing about the same topic at the time and take part in some kind of "national discussion."

People who read the standard version of *The Way of Men* that starts out proclaiming that "The Way of Men is the Way of the Gang" might assume that I hadn't spent years familiarizing myself with the arguments of feminists or the academic arguments about masculinity — but they would be wrong. I read what all of the "experts" like feminist sociologist Michael Kimmel, founder, and editor of the academic journal *Men and Masculinities*, had to say at the time.

Kimmel was eventually ruined and run out of academia in 2018 by sexual harassment allegations. But when I was writing *The Way of Men*, he was the guy that *The New York Times* and other media outlets would reach out to for "expert" commentary and feminist spin on any issue related to men or masculinity. So I engaged the arguments that Kimmel and his peers were making in a more innocent time when even a feminist university professor didn't have to specify (his?) pronouns.

When I finished the first draft of *The Way of Men*, I sent it off to a few associates. One of them was the writer Scott Locklin, who still occasionally writes for his blog "Locklin on Science."[1] Scott sent the draft back to me, and said, "It don't read good." Then he elaborated and told me it seemed to be more about what other people said than what I was saying. He advised me to cut all of that out and just say what I wanted to say without referencing all of those other people. Man, that was good advice, and I would give that advice to any writer today. Just say what you have to say. Your work shouldn't read like a Twitter thread. None of the great books read like that — just the "book of the week" shuffled

---

1   https://www.scottlocklin.wordpress.com

out every so often to make some journalist or columnist or pundit a few bucks and get them on some talk shows. No one remembers those books. I was writing about Hanna Rosin's article turned TED talk that eventually became the book titled *The End of Men*, which came out the same year as *The Way of Men*. Unless you were following the mainstream media in 2011/2012, you've probably never heard of it. She got all of the attention in the world at the time, but no one is reading that book now.

As much as I hated the idea of rewriting the book, Locklin was right. I cut all of that material out and eventually released it for free online as an e-book titled *No Man's Land*.

No Man's Land has been included in French and Italian editions of *The Way of Men*. I decided to include it here as well, and I think it is an important work in its own right. It is where I "show my work."

I often refer people to *No Man's Land* online when they are outraged about some feminist headline or magazine cover or public statement. What feminists have to say about men and masculinity and what they want men to do and give up for them and how they want men to change has been very consistent for several decades. Their demands always require, first, a "redefinition" or "reimagining" of masculine ideals in such a way that the concepts associated with masculinity are be placed in the service of feminist ideology. But ultimately, the end goal advanced by the transsexual transhumanism that unnaturally blossomed from feminism is to eliminate masculinity as a concept altogether.

No Man's Land provides a foundation for understanding the history of this discussion for the layman, as most men are completely unfamiliar with the arcana of feminist. *No Man's Land* is valuable and useful, I believe, in showing men that today's headlines are not new or shocking aberrations, but simply another repackaging of the same ideas that have been progressively advanced by feminist activists for at least half a century.

While the essay doesn't make this point specifically when you know that what they call "toxic masculinity" in 2022 was called "testosterone poisoning" in 1975, it gives you a certain sense of perspective.

ADDITIONAL NOTES

Unless I happened to catch a typo or missing word, I didn't edit or make many significant changes to the text of *The Way of Men* itself. I added a few additional notes, and those additions are indicated clearly in the Endnotes.

I did change the first sentence of the Preface. In the first edition, it read, "I present this book to you without ego." That was actually a riff on a line from one of Tarantino's *Kill Bill* films, spoken by Japanese sword smith, Hattori Hanzo.

> "I've created, "something that kills people." And in that purpose, I was a success. I've done this because, philosophically, I am sympathetic to your aim. I can tell you with no ego; this is my finest sword. If on your journey, you should encounter God, God will be cut."

Since then, I've bristled at the way the word "ego" — which really just means "I" in Latin — is used and misused as a "catch-all" for all self-acknowledgment, positive or negative, and the idea that true wisdom and achievement comes from "killing your ego." I'm a stickler for words and definitions. When men today say "ego," they usually mean "arrogance" or "hubris." So I changed the sentence to read, "I present this book without arrogance or hubris," in an attempt to better convey what I actually meant at the time.

I explained my objection to what I see as the misuse and misunderstanding of the word "ego" in a 2019 essay titled, "'This Is Your Captain Speaking' – In Defense of Ego," which is currently available on my website.[2]

2   https://www.jack-donovan.com/sowilo/2019/06/27/this-is-your-captain-speaking-in-defense-of-ego/

VIOLENCE IS GOLDEN

A lot of people like to think they are "non-violent." Generally, people claim to "abhor" the use of violence, and violence is viewed negatively by most folks. Many fail to differentiate between just and unjust violence. Some especially vain, self-righteous types like to think they have risen above the nasty, violent cultures of their ancestors. They say that "violence isn't the answer." They say that "violence doesn't solve anything."

They're wrong. Every one of them relies on violence, every single day.

On election day, people from all walks of life line up to cast their ballots, and by doing so, they hope to influence *who* gets to wield the axe of authority. Those who want to end violence — as if that were possible or even desirable — often seek to disarm their fellow citizens. This does not actually end violence. It merely gives the state mob a monopoly on violence. This makes you "safer," so long as you don't piss off the boss.

All governments — left, right or other — are by their very nature coercive. They have to be.

Order demands violence.

A rule not ultimately backed by the threat of violence is merely a suggestion. States rely on laws enforced by men ready to do violence against lawbreakers. Every tax, every code and every licensing requirement demands an escalating progression of penalties that, in the end, must result in the forcible seizure of property or imprisonment by armed men prepared to do violence in the event of resistance or non-compliance. Every time a soccer mom stands up and demands harsher penalties for drunk driving, or selling cigarettes to minors, or owning a pit bull, or not recycling, she is petitioning the state to use *force* to impose her will. She is no longer asking nicely. The viability of every family law, gun law, zoning law, traffic law, immigration law, import law, export law, and financial regulation depends on both the willingness and wherewithal of the group to exact order by force.

When an environmentalist demands that we "save the whales," he or she is in effect making the argument that saving the whales is so important that it is worth doing harm to humans who harm whales. The peaceful environmentalist is petitioning the leviathan to authorize the use of violence in the interest of protecting leviathans. If state leaders were to agree and express that it was, indeed, important to "save the whales," but then decline to penalize those who bring harm to whales, or decline to enforce those penalties under threat of violent police or military action, the expressed sentiment would be a meaningless gesture. Those who wanted to bring harm to whales would feel free to do so, as it is said, with impunity — without punishment.

Without action, words are just words. Without violence, laws are just words.

Violence isn't the only answer, but it is the final answer.

One can make moral arguments and ethical arguments and appeals to reason, emotion, aesthetics, and compassion. People are certainly moved by these arguments, and when sufficiently persuaded –providing of course that they are not excessively inconvenienced — people often choose to moderate or change their behaviors.

However, the willful submission of many inevitably creates a vulnerability waiting to be exploited by any one person who shrugs off social and ethical norms. If every man lays down his arms and refuses to pick them up, the first man to pick them up can do whatever he wants. Peace can only be maintained without violence so long as everyone sticks to the bargain, and to maintain peace, every single person in every successive generation — even after war is long forgotten — must continue to agree to remain peaceful. Forever and ever. No delinquent or upstart may ever ask, "*Or Else What?*," because in a truly non-violent society, the best available answer is "Or else we won't think you're a very nice person and we're not going to share with you." Our troublemaker is free to reply, "I don't care. I'll *take* what I want."

Violence is the final answer to the question, "*Or else what?*"

Violence is the gold standard, the reserve that guarantees order. In actuality, it is better than a gold standard, because violence has universal value. Violence transcends the quirks of philosophy, religion, technology, and culture. People say that music is a universal language, but a punch in the face hurts the same no matter what language you speak or what kind of music you prefer. If you are trapped in a room with me, and I grab a pipe and gesture to strike you with it, no matter who you are, your monkey brain will immediately understand "*or else what.*" And thereby, a certain order is achieved.

The practical understanding of violence is as basic to human life and human order as is the idea that fire is hot. You can use it, but you must respect it. You can act against it, and you can sometimes control it, but you can't just wish it away. Like wildfire, sometimes it is overwhelming, and you won't know it is coming until it is too late. Sometimes it is bigger than you. Ask the Cherokee, the Inca, the Romanovs, the Jews, the Confederates, the barbarians, and the Romans. They all know "*Or else what.*"

The basic acknowledgement that order demands violence is not a revelation, but to some it may seem like one. The very notion may make some people apoplectic, and some will furiously attempt to dispute it with all sorts of convoluted and hypothetical arguments, because it doesn't sound very "nice." But something doesn't need to be "nice" in order for it to be true. Reality doesn't bend over to accommodate fantasy or sentimentality.

Our complex society relies on proxy violence to the extent that many average people in the private sector can wander through life without really having to understand or think deeply about violence, because we are removed from it. We can afford to perceive it as a distant, abstract problem to be solved through high-minded strategy and social programming. When violence comes knocking, we simply make a call, and the police come to "stop" the violence. Few civilians really take the time to think that what we are essentially doing is paying an armed band protection money to come and do orderly violence on our behalf. When those who would do violence to us are taken peacefully, most of us don't really make the connection; we don't even *assert to ourselves* that the reason a perpetrator allows himself to be arrested is because of the gun on the officer's hip or the implicit understanding that he will eventually be hunted down by more officers who have the authority to kill him if he is deemed a threat. That is, if he is deemed a threat to *order*.

There are something like two and a half million people incarcerated in the United States. Over ninety percent of them are men. Most of them did not turn themselves in. Most of them don't try to escape at night because there is someone in a guard tower ready to shoot them. Many are "non-violent" offenders. Soccer moms, accountants, celebrity activists, and free range vegans all send in their tax dollars, and by proxy, spend billions and billions to feed an armed government that maintains order through violence.

It is when our *ordered violence* gives way to *disordered violence*, as in the aftermath of a natural disaster, that we are forced to see how much we rely on those who maintain order through violence. People loot because they can, and kill because they think they'll get away with it. Dealing with violence and finding violent men who will protect you from other violent men suddenly becomes a real and pressing concern.

A pal once told me a story about an incident recounted by a family friend who was a cop, and I think it gets the point across. A few teenagers were at the mall hanging out, outside a bookstore. They were goofing around and talking with some cops who were hanging around. The cop was a relatively big guy, not someone who you would want to mess around with. One of the kids told the cop that he didn't see why society needed police.

The cop leaned over and said to the spindly kid, "do you have any doubt in your mind about whether or not I could break your arms and take that book away from you if I felt like it?"

The teenager, obviously shaken by the brutality of the statement, said, "No."

"That's why you need cops, kid."

George Orwell wrote in his "Notes on Nationalism" that, for the pacifist, the truth that, "Those who 'abjure' violence can only do so because others are committing violence on their behalf," is obvious but impossible to accept. Much unreason flows from the inability to accept our passive reliance on violence for protection.

Escapist fantasies of the John Lennon "Imagine" variety corrupt our ability to see the world as it is and be honest with ourselves about the naturalness of violence to the human animal. There is no evidence to support the idea that man is an inherently peaceful creature. There is substantial evidence to support the notion that violence has always been a part of human life. Every day, archeologists unearth another primitive skull with damage from weapons or blunt force trauma. The very first legal codes were shockingly grisly. If we feel less threatened today, if we feel as though we live in a non-violent society, it is only because we have ceded so much power over our daily lives to the state. Some call this reason, but we might just as well call it laziness. A dangerous laziness, it would seem, given how little most people say they trust politicians.

Violence doesn't come from movies or video games or music. Violence comes from people. It's about time people woke up from their 1960s haze and started being honest about violence again. People are violent, and that's OK. You can't legislate it away or talk your way around it. Based on the available evidence, there's no reason to believe that world peace will ever be achieved, or that violence can ever be "stopped."

It's time to quit worrying and learn to love the battle axe. History teaches us that if we don't, someone else will.

*Originally published on Arthur's Hall of Viking Manliness (now offline),
Nov 11, 2010.*

NO MAN'S LAND

2012. Originally published online.

Part 1 – "No Man's Land"

If you were a science fiction writer freelancing for a men's magazine in the 1940s, you might have dreamed up a lurid dystopian future where women rule. You might have described a "New Girl Order," or titled your tale "The End of Men." For your bizarro tomorrow, you may well have envisioned a world where boys were punished, drugged, or expelled from school for the kinds of things you remembered doing as a kid. Males would be referred to as "the second sex," regarded as "louts," and relegated to low-paid, low-status jobs. Women would be sexually promiscuous, even marching together as "proud sluts[1]," while men would be legally required to ask for explicit verbal permission for every kiss.[2] When it came time to reproduce, females would often raise children (hopefully female children) on their own. Fathers would be considered quaint but ultimately

---

1   Melnick, Meredith. "From Legal Defense to Rallying Cry: How 'SlutWalks' Became a Global Movement." *Time* 10 May 2011. Web. 23 May 2011. http://healthland.time. com/2011/05/10/from-legal-defense-to-rallying-cry-how-slutwalks-became-a-global-movement

2   "The Antioch College Sexual Offense Prevention Policy." Antioch College. N.p., 1 Jan. 2006. Web. 23 May 2011. http://antiochmedia.org/mirror/antiwarp/www.antioch-college.edu/Campus/sopp/index.html

disposable.

Your readers, back then, would have had quite a chuckle.

However, if writers for America's major newspapers and magazines are to be believed, that future is not far off. While their phrasing could be a touch fantastic, and things may not yet be quite as bad as they say, there seems to be a growing consensus that unless major changes occur, the future is no man's land.

In May of 2000, Christina Hoff Sommers challenged the prevailing wisdom about sex and education when she wrote for *The Atlantic* that it was, "a bad time to be a boy in America."[3] Throughout the 1980s and 90s, feminist authors including Carol Gilligan and Mary Pipher had convinced educators that schools favored boys and shortchanged girls. Sommers made the case that, perhaps at least in part in response to overzealous attempts to help girls achieve parity, the evidence showed that girls were actually getting better grades and had higher educational aspirations than boys. Boys were dominating "drop out lists, failure lists, and learning-disability lists." Girls appeared to be more "engaged" in the educational process. Boys were still scoring better on some standardized tests (like the SAT), but this was because few "at-risk" boys were even bothering to take the test. According to Sommers, the partisans of girls were writing the rules, programs to aid boys had a very low priority, and the gender gap in academic achievement was widening.

Businessweek published a cover story in 2003 confirming "The New Gender Gap." Michelle Conlin claimed that boys were becoming "the second sex" from kindergarten to grad school. She reiterated Sommers' conclusions and described a bleak educational landscape where boys were being labeled as

---

3   Hoff Sommers, Christina. "The War Against Boys." *The Atlantic.* May 2000. Web. 2 Mar 2011. http://www.theatlantic.com/magazine/archive/2000/05/the-war-against-boys/4659/

troublemakers or "touchers," and a disturbing number were being diagnosed with Attention Deficit Hyperactivity Disorder. Conlin identified what she called a "creeping pattern of male disengagement and economic dependency" that started in youth and snowballed through adolescence, the college years (or comparative lack thereof), a declining male voting rate, and professional underachievement.[4] In the same issue, Thomas Mortenson, a senior scholar at the Pell Institute for the Study of Opportunity in Higher Education, told Conlin that the "new economy" was "a world made for women."[5]

Peg Tyre followed up for Newsweek in 2006, and found that things had only gotten worse for boys in education. From 1980 to 2001, the number of boys who said they didn't like school rose 71% in a study conducted by the University of Michigan. When her piece was published, males had become a minority on college campuses, representing just 44% of the student body.

I was able to observe some of this first hand when I was asked to participate in a "21st Century Manhood" workshop at a nearby private high school. The school was co-ed and extremely liberal, but the workshop was boys-only. It was well attended, and the boys had a lot to say. While the boys were clearly economically privileged, their female peers were too, so in their world-class wasn't a factor. There was a general consensus that the young men felt like wherever they turned, even when it came to athletics, "everything was about what the girls wanted." The teen movie jock vs. nerds status hierarchy also seemed to be inverted. It was the natural "alphas" of the group who seemed to be the most frustrated and disenfranchised. They told me that they were constantly being corrected and told what to say and how to feel. While feminists frequently claim masculinity is

4   Conlin, Michelle. "The New Gender Gap." Businessweek 26 May 2003. Web. 23 May 2011. http://www.businessweek.com/magazine/content/03_21/b3834001_mz001.htm

5   Conlin, Michelle. "This Is a World Made for Women." Businessweek 26 May 2003. Web. 23 May 2011 http://www.businessweek.com/magazine/content/03_21/b3834010_mz001.htm

merely a role that men "perform," and that feminism frees men from having to conform to an unrealistic ideal, it was clear to me that these boys felt as though they had to watch everything they said and did, and that they never felt they could simply "be themselves."

Media consultant Guy Garcia wrote that, "If men were a brand, their value would be dropping, because society is simply not buying what they're selling."[6] In his 2008 book, *The Decline of Men*, he argued that men were preoccupied with outdated expectations and "hypermasculine" rituals of violence, and that while women were attaining more academic credentials and making more money, men were "opting out, coming apart, and falling behind."[7] He imagined a future when, in a romantic role reversal, men who wanted to get married would end up waiting hopefully by the phone for Ms. Right to call, because men may have very little to offer their affluent, career-oriented female prospects. However, Garcia also worried that men might "yank at their chains and pull the entire temple down with them."[8]

In the same year, pro-feminist sociologist Michael Kimmel warned parents about the lure of "guyland."[9] Frat boys, the young men who in decades past would have been preparing to pursue careers and get married, were becoming less interested in doing either. According to Kimmel, "guys" were postponing those traditional markers of adulthood well into their thirties. He acknowledged that the media showed married men begging for sex and being routinely "infantilized" by their wives.[10] Kimmel wrote, "If that's your idea of adulthood, of marriage, and of family life, it makes sense that you'd want to postpone it for

---

6   Garcia, Guy. *The Decline of Men*. 2008. HarperCollins e-books. Loc. 738. Kindle.

7   Ibid. Loc 77.

8   Ibid. Loc 4190.

9   Kimmel, Micheal. *Guyland*. 2008. HarperCollins e-books. Kindle.

10   Ibid. Loc. 591.

as long as possible, or at least take the time to figure out a way to avoid the pitfalls so that your own life doesn't turn out that way." He observed that guys were often living in clusters together well after college, perpetuating frat life, working "McJobs," drinking, gambling, and "hooking up" with girls for casual sex. Kimmel explained that while young women were coming of age excited about their prospects and believing anything was possible for them, more and more young men were becoming addicted to sports, porn, and video games.

By 2009, there was growing evidence that boys were falling behind in school, and that many young men were more interested in partying, getting laid, or goofing off than they were in getting married or investing in their own futures. Women were doing well and men were having fun and everyone was making money, so most people didn't really care too much.

However, two events brought "the decline of men" into the spotlight.

The first was what has become known as "the great recession." The severe economic downturn of the late double-oughts included a real estate bust that resulted in layoffs and work shortages that disproportionately affected men in construction and related industries. The term "man-cession" became popular to describe a substantial gap in unemployment between men and women. Men were losing their jobs at a disproportionate rate, and projected job growth pointed to female-dominated service-sector industries like healthcare.

The second event that brought attention to the trouble with men was a milestone for women. In late 2009, women were poised to claim over half of the workforce. Maria Shriver and the Center for American Progress released a triumphant report, titled A

Woman's Nation Changes Everything[11], which named women "The New Breadwinners." Oprah Winfrey wrote an epilogue to the report, which told women it was up to them to turn the world "right side up." The Economist put Rosie the Riveter on its cover, and announced that in a "quiet revolution," women were "taking over the workplace" in what was "arguably the biggest social change of our times."[12]

In 2010, Hanna Rosin claimed in *The Atlantic* that it might be "The End of Men," and asked if modern, postindustrial society was simply better suited to women. Rosin wrote that for every two men who earn a B.A. degree, three women will earn one, and that in the fifteen job categories projected to grow in the United States, all but two were already dominated by women. She mused that, "the U.S. economy is in some ways becoming a kind of traveling sisterhood: upper-class women leave home and enter the workforce, creating domestic jobs for other women to fill." Even working-class women seem to be running the show at home, as fathers were increasingly absent or simply irrelevant— stripped of authority in household matters because they weren't earning as much as their wives or "partners." And for the first time in history, couples all over the world—even in once strictly patriarchal South Korea—are more often hoping for baby girls. [13]

For *Newsweek*, Andrew Romano and Tony Doupkil complained that even though women were making more money, men were still doing half as much housework and avoiding "girly" jobs in the booming healthcare industry because they were

11   Shriver, Maria. "The Shriver Report: A Woman's Nation Changes Everything." *The Center for American Progress*. The Center for American Progress, 16 Oct. 2009. Web. 24 May 2011. http://www.americanprogress.org/issues/2009/10/womans_nation.html

12   "We did it!." *The Economist*. N.p., 30 Dec. 2009. Web. 24 May 2011. http://www.economist.com/node/15174489?story_id=1517448

13   Rosin, Hanna. "The End of Men." *The Atlantic*. July 2010. Web. 24 Feb. 2011. http://www.theatlantic.com/magazine/archive/2010/07/the-end-of-men/8135/

sticking to a "musty script of masculinity."[14] In the *Los Angeles Times*, Neal Gabler wrote that modern men had become "louts," and concluded that "in a world of unrelenting pressures and of threatening sexual equality, men just want to be boys."[15] Days later, in *The Wall Street Journal*, Kay Hymowitz wondered where all the "good men" had gone. By "good men," like Garcia and the others, she seemed to mean a financially successful man who was willing to leave his male friends and the activities they enjoyed—sports, video games, gadgets, action films and sex with multiple women—to commit to a woman and help her raise a family (for as long as she wanted him to).[16]

Women want men to compete with them in the workplace, yet cooperate with them for the purposes of reproduction. Anthropologist Lionel Tiger identified this source of "substantial tension in" his 1999 book, *The Decline of Males*.[17] Indeed, The Decline of Males predicted many of the problems that the writers above have been hashing through over the past decade. Playing on the words of Marx, Tiger understood that men were not only becoming alienated from the means of production but also from the means of reproduction.[18] The invention of the birth control pill, combined with the rise of feminism, the industrial/information economy, and the welfare state had produced a "single-mother system." State intervention, intended to help children in need, had created a new kind of family: the bureaugamy. Tiger defined bureaugamy as "a family pattern involving a mother, a child, and a bureaucrat."[19]

---

14   Romano, Andrew, and Tony Doupkil. "Men's Lib." *Newsweek*. 20 Sept. 2010. Web. 24 Feb. 2011. http://www.newsweek.com/2010/09/20/why-we-need-to-reimagine-masculinity.html

15   Gabler, Neal. "Day of the Lout." *Los Angeles Times*. 13 Feb. 2011. Web. 24 Feb. 2011. http://www.latimes.com/entertainment/news/la-ca-louts-20110213,0,2024755.story

16   Hymowitz, Kay S. "Where Have The Good Men Gone?" *The Wall Street Journal*. 19 Feb. 2011. Web. 24 Feb. 2011. http://online.wsj.com/article/SB10001424052748704409004576146321725889448.html

17   Tiger, Lionel. *The Decline of Males*. 1999. Golden Books. Print. 233.

18   Ibid. 249.

19   Ibid. 159.

The patriarchal kinship system that demanded paternal investment was dismantled by feminists, technology and the legal system. It was replaced with a system that gave women control over virtually all aspects of reproduction, and where a woman could rest assured that the state would step in and provide for her children in the absence of a husband or father. Divorce, most often initiated by women, offered a way for women to seize control of their families at-will, even when a man had chosen to make a paternal investment. Men had become peripheral players in the lives of their offspring, and they could be cut from the team by coach mom at any time. The managing bureaucrat would then determine what role the father would have in his children's lives—at best he might be offered a co-parenting role, at worst he could be reduced to a mere paycheck.

America may not yet be a matriarchy, but her family structure has become matrilineal, or at least matrifocal. The practice of giving a child his or her father's surname is a vestigial gesture, an outdated social norm from an earlier time. If women were to stop doing it altogether, or if they were to insist that their names come first in a mother-hyphen-father configuration, any enduring illusion of patriarchy would be shattered. One has to wonder if, in the absence of that illusion, men would invest in fatherhood at all. The switch to a bonobo culture—where males are mere inseminators and helpers—would at that point be explicit and complete. Why wouldn't men simply shuffle about alone or in small, impotent groups, playing games and seeking masturbatory short-term gratification? Why would they make the investment or the sacrifices necessary to be good husbands and fathers, when a woman could take it all away on a whim?

None of the scolds have managed to come up with a plan for getting young "guys" to stop drinking, hooking up or playing video games, and start families instead. All they've managed to do in exhorting men to "man up" is invoke the "musty script" of a patriarchal system that no longer exists.

To Kay Hymowitz's credit, in her book titled *Manning Up: How the Rise of Women Has Turned Men into Boys,* she also recognized that there were "demographic, economic, technological, cultural—and hormonal"[20] reasons why males have been falling behind or opting out, and why for the first time ever, "young women are reaching their twenties with more achievements, more education, more property, and, arguably, more ambition than their male counterparts."[21] She shrewdly noted that it was not only feminism, but also the Playboy mentality[22] that had worked to erode the love-marriage-baby carriage moral and social prescription that, for so long, encouraged young men to think seriously about their careers and marriage from an early age. More than the others, she also sympathized with the much maligned American male—stuck staring down life in the "cold intimacy"[23] of a domesticated office and treated like a disposable putz.

Hymowitz wondered, "where do boys fit into the girl-powered world?"[24]

She didn't have an answer. Most seem to shrug their shoulders. Some talk and write about making the educational system more boy-friendly. That couldn't hurt.

The writers above agree, for the most part, that few industries in any peaceful, global, post-industrial economy favor the aptitudes or the temperament of males. However, as we will see, the very idea that males have a natural temperament chafes against established biases toward cultural determinism and the orthodoxy of feminist sex role theory.

---

20   Hymowitz, Kay. *Manning Up: How the Rise of Women Has Turned Men into Boys.* 2011. Basic Books. Kindle. Loc. 1558

21   Ibid. Loc. 819.

22   Ibid. Loc. 1837.

23   Ibid. Loc. 1910.

24   Ibid. Loc. 1035.

Instead of critically evaluating our society's plans for the future and trying to create a system that is better for both sexes, most writers have simply demanded that men change their temperaments.

Masculinity, the theory goes, can be whatever we want it to be—so why not "reimagine" a masculinity that better suits the future?

Part 2 – "Reimagining Masculinity"

"A beast of prey tamed and in captivity—every zoological garden can furnish examples—is mutilated, world-sick, inwardly dead. Some of them voluntarily hunger-strike when they are captured. Herbivores give up nothing in being domesticated."

—Oswald Spengler, *Man and Technics*

Today, many people would consider it cruel to place an animal in an enclosure that is drastically different from its natural habitat. We design our zoos and aquariums and terrariums to simulate natural conditions as best we can. Enthusiastic hobbyists spend small fortunes attempting to create miniature facsimiles of the natural world. This is to "please" their captive fauna. Although many suppose that the animal would be "happier" in the wild, insofar as animals experience "happiness," most seem to believe that animals are dumb enough to be tricked into being reasonably content in a half-assed knock-off of the ecosystem they were snatched from. So we spruce up a small glass box with coral to make it feel like the ocean, or hang a garland of palm leaves and call it the jungle. Most animals really aren't that bright, so maybe it is just as well for Mr. Fish to swim around the ceramic pirate ship so long as he is reasonably safe and his belly is full.

Getting men, especially young men, to adapt to the confines and limitations of civilized society has always been a bit of a challenge. Virile restlessness, athleticism, and competitiveness have been trained and tamed by sports and games throughout history. Gaming has provided the shoemaker and bricklayer with the feel of conflict, danger, and war in peaceful, prosperous times. People always assumed that men were drawn to certain kinds of activities, and that providing some sort of release valve for natural male aggression was healthy. It made men happy to do the things they wanted to do, and ways were found for men to exert their virility constructively—or with minimal destruction.

For most men, even "civilized" work was more challenging and demanded more physical exertion than it does now. Work was goal-oriented; it required skill and practical know-how. It provided a tangible, personal, and immediate sense of purpose. Farming, blacksmithing, and building can all easily be framed as symbolic struggles against nature. Work felt more like aggression and the exertion of will. On our continuum of masculinity, work was more direct and engaging, less removed from the primal struggle for survival.

The industrial revolution pulled men away from physically and mentally engaging trades and replaced those trades with simple jobs and tasks which required little skill or thought. Increasingly, work felt like submission. Sports become more popular and important than ever before. Hobbies like woodworking and hunting and various outdoor activities were promoted as manly pursuits. Men bought pulp magazines filled with lurid tales of exotic adventures they knew they'd never have. Men marveled at strongmen, then weightlifters, then bodybuilders. With decreased opportunities for virile action, men were increasingly drawn to opportunities for virile display. Masculinity became increasingly vicarious, virtual, and symbolic.

The transition to a service and "knowledge work" economy made things worse for men. The cubicle felt even less like active, aggressive work. Some men are particularly suited to it, or they manage to channel their energy elsewhere, but the "jobs of the future" leave a lot of men inwardly dead. The modern workplace often feels like a fishbowl without so much as a ceramic pirate ship to swim around. If anything, these days, it's a bunch of pink plastic flowers. If you accept the possibility that men and boys, like the males of most other large animals, have in general a different nature and a different set of reproductive interests than the female of the species, it is not difficult to see why the modern, post-feminist world has men "underperforming."

Unfortunately, when those in the media talk about men in the 21st century, the questions they ask and the answers they offer usually stink of false naiveté. Like the female reporter who, with a straight face, asked actor Charlie Sheen why he liked to have sex with porn stars, the media remains purposefully and self righteously clueless about the nature of men.

Feminists claimed the moral high ground, appealing to men's sense of fairness. They convinced men to help them reorganize society and eliminate the notion that males and females should have different sex roles and responsibilities. Men, perhaps egotistically, agreed that The Way of Men was better, and that it was unfair to prevent women from achieving their full potential in the way that men conceptualized both achievement and potential. Western wealth and technology made this social transformation possible. Manly virtues were neutered and simply became "virtues"— though the Latin root vir means "man." To make women feel equal and encourage them to achieve in the public realm, men were encouraged to change the way they talked about manhood. Strength, courage, and honor were de-sexed and reinterpreted in more relative terms. To be inclusive, people invented different "kinds" of strength, courage and honor, so that the weakest boy or the meekest girl could somehow feel strong, courageous, or honorable. As part of this massive self-esteem-building project for women, the idea of "emotional intelligence" was introduced and promoted, thought it was never really taken seriously. To explain women's historical lack of achievement, men as a sex were cast as mere bullies. The achievements of history's great men were reconsidered and judged according to standards determined by feminist ideology. Noble institutions and social clubs for men that encouraged civic responsibility and "moral masculinity" were renounced as exclusive and patriarchal, or forcibly integrated and rendered impotent and unrecognizable.

Women appropriated everything they wanted from thousands of years of male culture, and men cobbled together a collective identity from what was left—benign macho posturing, fart jokes, and beer. Now that imported or micro-brewed "craft" beer is becoming the new wine, and female politicians pose with guns and run around telling folks to "man up," I'm afraid all that men will have left is fart jokes. This is troubling to me because— despite the persistent efforts of flatulent friends—I still don't find fart jokes all that funny, much less a desirable basis for my "gender identity."

In 1974, feminist Janet Saltzman Chafetz imagined a utopia where androgyny replaced gender role stereotypes. She hoped that, perhaps by the year 2000, people would move beyond perceiving themselves as being either masculine or feminine, and instead see themselves as merely being human.[1] It is a theme in much of feminist writing that men and women must discover a common humanity and abandon old ideas about the sexes.

However, in the case of women, this has consistently been a case of saying one thing and doing another. Only men are expected to see the world in gender-neutral terms. Women organize consistently as a group to advocate for women's interests. Even as they have fought for inclusion in every realm once reserved for men, they have created an entire subculture catering specifically to women. As I write this, there is a women's film festival going on in my town. There are women's gyms, and a dizzying number of women's health and health advocacy organizations. Women have their own magazines, television channels, websites, bookstores, and so on. There is, as Hanna Rosin mentioned, a "traveling sisterhood" of women helping each other as women— not merely as human beings. Women are acting collectively in

---

1   Saltzman Chafetz, Janet. *Masculine, Feminine or Human?* 2nd ed. Itasca: Peacock Publishers, 1978. 221-58. Print.

their own interests as a sex.

Women have not abandoned their sexual identities; they have expanded them. Whereas men are told that they can no longer do the things they used to do, and are asked to repudiate their heritage as males, women are told to embrace their past, to keep doing everything that they've always done—and do more!

A common bumper sticker reads:

"Feminism is the radical notion that women are human beings."

It should read:

Feminism is the radical notion that men should do whatever women say, so that women can do whatever the hell they want.

The androgynous feminism of Chafetz has, in practice, become a feminism that sells women strength and power but permits them to maintain a distinct sexual identity and organize to advance their own interests as a sex. We have not become simply "human"—we still recognize ourselves as men and women, even in 2011. Chafetz acknowledged that feminism posed a threat to men, because the change would entail, "a loss of many concrete prerogatives."[2] She was right about that. By any straightforward measure, feminism required men to progressively transfer power to women. If advances in technology and global exchange had been slower, this transfer might have been more orderly and even-handed. However, in Chafetz's lifetime, economic and technological changes happened so rapidly that women were able to capitalize on them and transform the workplace and the social terrain to their liking at once, while men were left standing with their dicks in their hands.

---

2   Ibid. 246.

Guy Garcia hopes that this failure to adapt will liberate men—that, broken by economic and social change, men will remake themselves in the shadow of Amazonian triumph. At the Burning Man festival, he wondered, "What better way to welcome the resplendent return of the Goddess than with the symbolic immolation of the male?"[3] Garcia wrapped up *The Decline of Men* with the story of Gerald Levin, who was the architect of the disastrous AOL/Time Warner merger in 2000. When the merger failed, a reeling Levin started talking about bringing "the poetry" back into life during an interview with Lou Dobbs. Levin was approached by a much younger woman who wanted him to invest in a boutique wellness clinic catering to celebrities and other high-profile clients. Eventually, he left his wife of 32 years for his new business partner.[4] Levin moved to California, where he now serves as the Managing Director of the Moonview Sanctuary. The Moonview Sanctuary specializes in New Age therapy and holistic healing, and Levin has said it is now his mission to "break down male culture."[5]

The dubious notion that humans once roamed the earth in peaceful, goddess worshipping matriarchal tribes offered a way for feminists and pacifists to reimagine a masculinity completely unlike the strength and aggression-based masculinity that has been a relative constant throughout history. If people were once "naturally" peaceful, then all we know of human HIStory could be reframed as an aberration—a fever of male violence that swept over all people in every land. If people were once "naturally" peaceful, then feminism could be reframed as a return to the natural order of things, instead of a departure from nature. Evolutionary biologists Wrangham and Peterson convincingly argued that,

---

3   Garcia, Guy. *The Decline of Men*. N.p.: HarperCollins e-books. Loc. 4332. Kindle.

4   Stevenson, Seth. "The Believer." *New York Magazine*. 9 July 2007. Web. 24 Feb. 2011. http://nymag.com/news/features/34454/

5   Garcia, Guy. *The Decline of Men*. N.p.: HarperCollins e-books. Loc. 4436. Kindle.

"It is good to dream, but sober, waking rationality suggests that if we start with ancestors like chimpanzees and end up with modern humans building walls and fighting platforms, the 5-million-year-long-trail to our modern selves was lined, along its full stretch, by a male aggression that structured our ancestors' social lives and technology and minds."[6]

It is most likely that men, armed with greater upper body and overall strength, have used that strength to assert their own reproductive interests over the interests of women and other men in predictable and familiar patterns over and over again. Any other conclusion requires magical thinking.

Eco-pacifist Sam Keen also believed in a peaceful, matriarchal prehistory, and many of the ideas presented in his 1991 New York Times Bestseller *Fire in the Belly* rest on the assumption that the ideas we have about masculinity were shaped by a "warfare system" which followed agricultural development.[7] However, like Wrangham and Peterson, archaeologist Lawrence Keeley concluded in his grim catalog of pre-historic violence, *War Before Civilization*, that the notion of a pacified past is, "incompatible with the most relevant ethnographic and archaeological evidence."[8] If calls for a return to a feminine system are based on a peaceful pre-history that never was, then there is nothing to return to.

While some radical feminists, queer theorists, transgendered persons, and others have argued for the eradication of gender stereotypes and a move beyond perceiving people as being either masculine or feminine, the fact remains that biologically speaking about half of humans are male and the other half female.

---

6   Wrangham, Richard, and Dale Peterson. *Demonic Males : Apes and the Origins of Human Violence.* New York: Mariner Books/Houghton Mifflin Company, 1996. 172. Print.

7   Keen, Sam. *Fire in the Belly.* Bantam Books, 1992. 35-48, 88-111. Print.

8   Keeley, Lawrence H. *War Before Civilization.* Oxford University Press, 1996. 2338. Kindle.

Most people seem to be willing to accept the idea that males and females are at least somewhat different. Men and women still maintain and prefer distinct sexual identities.

Indeed, much of the 21st Century triumphalism about the rise of women and "The End of Men" acknowledges differences between the sexes and celebrates a distinct female identity.

The new way of women downplays the importance of physical differences between the sexes and praises women for their communication skills, their ability to multitask, and their preferences for social coalition building and non-violent conflict resolution. The new way of women celebrates female empowerment and the importance of women in shaping history, and chronicles their rise to prominence as a peaceful overcoming of oppression, guided by a desire for justice and equality. Women are taught to take pride in womanhood, and they expect to be able to do just about anything their heart desires.

The problem with the new way of women is that it relies on a transfer of power and opportunity from men, and if this power exchange is to last, men will have to be taught to downgrade their expectations, even as women are taught to expect the world. The new way of women called for a new way of men. Many have attempted to reimagine masculinity in a way that repudiates the old, violent patriarchal "myths" about men, and provides a more peaceful and sexually egalitarian vision of manhood that is compatible with what women want for themselves.

The mythopoetic men's movement attempted to do this in the 1980s and early 1990s. In *Iron John*, poet Robert Bly tapped into folklore and tried to help men get in touch with the "wild man." *Iron John* contained some truthful observations, and it got media attention when it was published in 1990. Feminists saw it as a kind of resurgent sexism and mocked it ruthlessly. In 1995, Michael Kimmel edited a collection of essays titled *The*

Politics of Manhood: Profeminist Men respond to the Mythopoetic Men's Movement (And the Mythopoetic Leaders Answer). Most of the essays were criticisms of *Iron John*. The profeminists accused Bly and company of everything from homophobia to male hysteria.[9]

Had they given Bly a fair read, they would have seen that his "wild man" was really quite tame. Bly's wild way was explicitly meant to exist in harmony with the feminist project. While it was incompatible with the sci-fi unitard androgyny of Chafetz's utopian feminism, Bly's ethos was a response to the way feminism had actually played out on the ground.

Bly stated in his response to profeminist men that it was important for men to "stand up and speak about the pain that millions of women feel" and that as a father, he wanted his daughters to have "a fair chance." He also denied charges that he or any of the mythopoetic men had any interest in reestablishing patriarchy, and even went on to say that the "destructive essence of patriarchy...moves to kill the young masculine."[10] Like other feminists and many men's rights activists, he believed that patriarchy hurts most men, too.

In *Iron John*, Bly wrote reverently about the power of the feminine in both myth and reality. His main concern was that men had grown softer and gentler, but that they had "not become more free"[11] because in the wake of feminist advances, many young men spent their lives working to please their mothers, girlfriends, and wives—while women were working to assert their power at home and at work. He blamed the Industrial revolution for separating boys from their fathers, creating a generation of males who learned "feeling primarily from the mother" and

---

9   Kimmel, Michael S., ed. *The Politics of Manhood : Profeminist Men Respond to the Mythopoetic Men's Movement* (And the Mythopoetic Leaders Answer). Temple University Press, 1995. Print.

10   Ibid. 272.

11   Bly, Robert. *Iron John*. Vintage Books. 1992. 2. Print.

learned to see manhood from the feminine point of view, and found themselves afraid or suspicious of their own masculinity.[12] This observation was astute, and this is likely to be the case for the increasing number of young men who are raised by single mothers. Men have always learned how to be men from older men, and Bly believed that as boys became increasingly distant from their fathers and grandfathers and other potentially positive mentors, they grew up unsure of themselves and uncomfortable in their own skin. His adapted myth of the "wild man" (an ancient, hairy, mysterious woodland mentor) was meant to help men deal with their primal nature and face the challenges of modernity with resolve, but never cruelty.[13]

Bly understood some of the problems men and boys were facing as they stood in the rubble of patriarchy, looking up to rising women. However, his solutions were forced, and his New Agey tone had limited appeal. The idea of grown men going out into the woods to sit in drum circles, read poetry and talk about their feelings was cringe-worthy. It also seemed spoiled and self indulgent. But the biggest problem with Bly's reimagining of masculinity was that it lacked balls.

Bly wrote of swords and battle, but his battles were the bloodless cartoon fantasies of the most innocent inner child, not the real, bloody conflicts of men. His use of myth was selectively biased in this direction. He cites Homer often and gives King Arthur as an example of a "male mother,"[14] but passes over the prominent themes of bloodlust and honor-seeking in the Iliad and the lurid orgies of smiting and beheading that peppered Malory's *Le Morte D'Arthur*. Bly advocates the cultivation of an inner warrior but belittles the men whose job it is to make war as mere "soldiers." Bly's new age "inner warrior" was told to assert himself, but

---

12   Ibid. 25.

13   Ibid. 8.

14   Ibid. 182.

he could only do so with words. He couldn't back it up. He was impotent.

In Bly's own words:

> "If a culture does not deal with the warrior energy—take it up consciously, discipline it, honor it—it will turn up outside in the form of street gangs, wife-beating, drug violence, brutality to children, and aimless murder.
>
> One major task of contemporary men is to reimagine, now that the images of eternal warrior and outward warrior no longer provide the model, the value of the warrior in relationships, in literary studies, in thought, in emotion."[15]

Bly's "inner warrior" never makes war, and can only survive in a state where he is protected from men who are prepared to use violence against other violent men. The world is still a violent place, and the inner warrior would be a joke—and a helpless target—in the ghetto or the Third World. Bly speaks from a pampered Western upper middle-class perspective, where people devote their time to "literary studies" and "relationships." The inner warrior attempts to make use of the vocabulary and the virtues that have characterized masculinity throughout history. Without the real-world rationales for strength, courage, and honor, he is left with a bunch of melodramatic metaphors for a mundane reality.

Sam Keen also attempted to reimagine masculinity by appropriating the language of violent masculinity for disarmed men. In *Fire In The Belly*, he told men to reject the "myth of war" and to become "fierce gentlemen." Keen's fierce gentleman really had nothing to distinguish himself from a fierce gentlewoman. His virtues were Wonder, Empathy, a Heartful Mind, Moral

---

15   Ibid. 179.

Outrage, Right Livelihood, Enjoyment, Friendship, Communion, Husbanding, and Wildness.[16] None of these are particularly bad values, but they aren't gendered concepts and they have nothing in particular to do with any historical sense of manhood. Feminists, to whom Keen genuflected numerous times, have been in the moral outrage business for years.

In his 1996 magnum opus, *Manhood in America*, Michael Kimmel hypocritically employed the script of traditional strength-based masculinity to shame Bly and Keen in his chapter on "Wimps, Whiners and Weekend Warriors."[17] Their attempts to nurture some meaningful connection to the myth and history of men— however carefully edited, pacified, and conciliatory to feminists in spirit—were still perceived as too much of a threat to the agendas of feminist activists and academics. As an alternative, Kimmel offered what he called a "democratic manhood." He defined this as "a gender politics of inclusion, of standing up against injustice based on difference," and suggested that men should embrace feminism, gay liberation, and multiculturalism as a blue-print for the reconstruction of masculinity.[18] Kimmel decorates his democratic manhood with a sense of struggle against adversity and vague feel of heroism, but calling this "manhood" is a crass and condescending manipulation. Kimmel's profeminist man is a no-man. His masculinity is defined by the rejection of traditional definitions of masculinity, save for its reliance on a narrative of self-sacrifice. This democratic no-man must renounce his own sense of identity and devote his energies to helping others attain a "sure and confident" sense of themselves and "their rightful share of the sun."[19] He must commit himself to selfless toil on behalf of others, and he must do so without question or complaint. Kimmel assures men that

---

16   Keen, Sam. *Fire in the Belly*. Bantam Books, 1992. 112-122, 152-185. Print.

17   Kimmel, Michael. *Manhood in America : A Cultural History*. The Free Press. 1996. 316-321. Print.

18   Ibid. 333.

19   Ibid. 334, 335.

somehow, by giving up the struggle to "prove manhood," men will finally be free, and be able to "breathe a collective sigh of relief."

If proving manhood is no longer necessary, what will motivate males to strive to prove that they are "democratic men?" Relieved of all but the most high-minded, abstract, and legally optional expectations, what is to stop men from collectively putting their feet up, breathing a sigh of relief, and doing...as little as possible?

The pacified, "reimagined" masculinities of Garcia, Bly, Keen, and Kimmel all require men to deny their own interests. The only carrots they dangle for men are obscure and philosophical and therefore naturally have a very limited appeal. Garcia, Bly, Keen, and Kimmel have nothing to say to the man who is looking for a way to better his own circumstances or make his own way in the material world.

Sensing that men are pacing their concrete cages, the reimaginers of masculinity have attempted to redecorate man's pound with questing narratives and talk of wildness. But a spiritual journey is just a story about thinking. You don't actually go anywhere. The inner warrior never knows what it means to face death head-on, or to see the life leave the eyes of his vanquished foe. His victories are petty, and his defeats are trivial. The weekend initiate to manhood never feels the earth on his knees, the urgency of hunger, or the warmth of fresh blood on his forehead. And the man who denies his own will to power so that others may thrive makes himself a slave.

Kimmel and other feminists frequently goad men who reject feminism and cosmopolitan values by accusing them of escapism and retreat. But the ascetic masculinity that feminists promote requires a retreat inward—guided by a near-religious and open-ended commitment to helping women, gays, and racial minorities achieve their own goals. Feminists and pacifists ask men to live passive lives of restraint and self-discipline. There have always been priests and monks and self-flagellators who got off on self denial. A certain kind of man, usually an intellectual, will find this lifestyle to his taste. Men generally seem to appreciate the obsessive fortitude required for internal as well as external battles. Abstinence has its own momentum, and tends to impart a sense of superiority over those who give in to primal appetites. But Kimmel and the others are blind solipsists if they believe a majority of men will ever become equally passionate about their pet projects, or that all men will be equally willing to put aside their own interests indefinitely.

Equality can't demand that one group restrain itself so that the other group can prosper and do whatever it wants. "Equality," if such a thing were even possible, would at least theoretically offer everyone the same opportunity to act in their own best interests as individuals, with limited interference from others.

However, like Diana Moon Glampers, the Handicapper General from Kurt Vonnegut's "Harrison Bergeron," organized feminists consistently demand a measurable equality of outcome. It has not been enough for women to gain an equality of opportunity.[20] If enough women aren't involved in sports or the sciences or if women aren't equally represented as generals and captains of industry, feminists demand that resources be diverted away from programs that help men, and advocate for programs that encourage women. Since the success of such programs can only be measured by the success of women in the desired area (whether they are succeeding or not) any self-interested bureaucrat who wants to please his or her superiors had better have the numbers to prove men and women are equal every which way. The net effect in such scenarios is always a soft discrimination against men. The hypocrisy of feminists when it comes to "equality-seeking"

---

20   Vonnegut,   Kurt.   "Harrison   Bergeron."   *National   Review.*   16
Nov.   1965.   Web.   26   Mar.   2011.   http://www.nationalreview.com/
nroriginals/?q=MDllNmVmNGU1NDVjY2IzODBlMjYzNDljZTMzNzFlZjc

efforts is evident from their apparent disinterest in rolling back programs which have made women more successful than men in a given field of endeavor, and in their vocal resistance to starting programs that help men in areas where men are lagging. The "equality" script is employed by women when it serves their interests, but many take a more punitive tone when it comes to lifting the bags of birdshot from the necks of men. After all, men deserve their handicaps for oppressing women. Men born in the wake of second-wave feminism are punished for the supposed sins of their long-dead forefathers.

Although profeminists from Keen to Kimmel attribute women with the noblest and most innocent equality-seeking aims, the truth is that women are neither good nor evil. They are simply female primates, who, like the male of the species, will band together and skew things to their liking if given the opportunity. Women are ascendant, and they have no intention of making any changes that might compromise their advancements. They will err on the side of caution and make sure they are always a little more equal than men whenever it really counts. Not because women are evil, but because they will serve their own interests first.

There's a concept within the "men's movement" known as "Men Going Their Own Way" (MGTOW). It is a feminist concept in the sense that the MGTOW manifesto generally acknowledges the rights of women to vote and do what they want and does not seek to reestablish patriarchy. The MGTOW movement more or less encourages men to serve their own immediate interests and to do whatever they want, too. It is a decentralized movement that advises men to work against feminist laws that favor women or unfairly penalize men.[21] The basic idea is simply, "you go your way, and I'll go mine."

---

21   "MEN GOING THEIR OWN WAY ver. 2.2." *Men For Justice*. N.p., 9 May 2006. Web. 13 Mar. 2011. http://menforjustice.net/cms/index.php?option=com_content&task=view&id=5&Itemid=4

While relatively few men would recognize the MGTOW acronym, it is true that many young men are "going their own way." And that's exactly what feminists like Rosin, Kimmel, Garcia, Romano, Doupkil, Gabler, and Hymowitz have been fretting about. While there will always be exceptions—the ascetics and the passive, herbivorous[22] "bonobo" boys—young men who were raised by women, processed through a feminist-friendly educational system, who see that women probably have better prospects than they do, and who have been relieved of the responsibilities associated with patriarchy see no reason to toil to help women get the things they want, especially in a society that aspires to "equality" between the sexes. As Rosin and others trumpet a future where girls are for the first time more desirable than boys, they must see the gall in asking men to get excited about speeding the plow.

Young men are becoming cynical and distrustful of a system that is designed to favor everyone but them. Scolding lectures from the agents of diversity culture that tell young men they are simply reacting to a loss of "privilege" certainly don't inspire them to invest in a future where they have even less "privilege"—especially if it seems likely that this future will "privilege" everybody else.

Young men who see no reason to invest in the future are doing what they always do—they're thinking short term and taking whatever they can get in the present.

Mark Simpson coined the term "metrosexual" in a 1994 essay, "Here Come the Mirror Men," to describe a rising male narcissism evident from consumer trends in Western nations. These men, too, were "going their own way"—working out, shopping for

22   Otagaki, Yumi. "Japan's "herbivore" men shun corporate life, sex." *Reuters*. N.p., 27 July 2009. Web. 13 Mar. 2011. http://www.reuters.com/article/2009/07/27/us-japan-herbivores-idUSTRE56Q0C220090727

fashionable clothes, and grooming themselves to attract women (or men) by virtue of their appearances instead of their virility, their accomplishments or their ability to provide economically. Simpson has mused that these "mirror men" were more likely to be in love with themselves than with a woman.[23]

These young men have discovered that good grooming and the appearance of affluence is not all they need to get laid. Pick up artists and advocates of "game" like the pseudonymous authors of the popular blog Citizen Renegade (now "Heartiste") advise men to take advantage of evolutionary psychology and appear to be "alpha"—a primal group leader—when dealing with women. Game advocates say that a man can run game inside a marriage or a long-term relationship, but they generally take a dim view of a married man's chances for well-being and fulfillment—especially financial well-being and sexual fulfillment.[24] Game as a sexual strategy seems to be geared toward providing short term gratification for men and women, but also avoiding long term misery. As my colleague W.F. Price at *The Spearhead* has written, there are no more wives—or at least there are very few. Young women no longer grow up preparing for everyday married life; they grow up planning their careers, their wardrobes, and their gauzy, frosted Cinderella fantasy weddings.[25]

There have also been changes in the sexual economy that satisfy the short-term sexual interests of young men. As Tiger noted, available contraception changed almost everything. Women hold more cards in terms of long-term options. Young men know that a pregnant woman can choose to abort or not without input

---

23   Simpson, Mark. "Here Come The Mirror Men." *Independent* 15 Nov. 1994 [UK]. Web. 13 Mar. 2011. http://www.marksimpson.com/pages/journalism/mirror_men.html

24   Chateau. "Game And Life Trajectory." *Citizen Renegade*. N.p., 24 Feb. 2011. Web. 13 Mar. 2011. http://heartiste.wordpress.com/2011/02/24/game-and-life-trajectory/(Updated link)

25   Price, W.F. "Stop Looking For a Wife: You Won't Find One." *The Spearhead*. N.p., 8 Oct. 2010. Web. 21 Mar. 2011. http://www.the-spearhead.com/2010/10/08/stop-looking-for-a-wife-you-wont-find-one. 2021 NOTE - *The Spearhead* is long since offline.

from him, and she can demand child support if she chooses to keep her baby. If he has chosen to make the long-term investment in a family, he knows that a woman—women initiate the majority of divorces—may leave him and demand child support at any time. But when it comes to getting short-term sexual gratification, so long as birth control is employed, "the market 'price' of sex is currently very low."[26] In the past, premarital sex had high social costs (especially for women), and the social costs of out-of-wedlock birth were even higher. However, now that premarital sex has become a norm, contraceptives are widely available, and young women are more likely to be financially successful or self-sufficient, they can afford to demand less long term commitment from men in return for sex. If they demand more, there are other girls who will demand less, and they will be priced out of the market. According to a recent article in Slate, this is exactly what is happening, especially on college campuses where there are more females than males. These young women are "are more negative about campus men, hold more negative views of their relationships, go on fewer dates, are less likely to have a boyfriend, and receive less commitment in exchange for sex." A National Longitudinal Study of Adolescent Health showed that sex was happening sooner in relationships, and that 30% of young men's relationships, "involve no romance at all: no wooing, no dates, no nothing."[27]

Michael Kimmel noted similar campus trends in his book, *Guyland.* He blamed the boys for the fact that the girls have gone wild—"hooking up" promiscuously instead of dating, because that's what the boys want. It is interesting that even as Kimmel claimed young women have the world on the string, he more or less admitted that they are so desperate for male attention that they'll gladly debauch themselves for it. Kimmel validated the alpha vs. beta worldview of "game" theorists when he wrote:

26   Regnerus, Mark. "Sex Is Cheap." *Slate.* 25 Feb 2011. Web. 16 Mar. 2011. http://www.slate.com/id/2286240/pagenum/all/#p2

27   Ibid.

> "Women sustain Guyland because Guyland seems to be populated by Rhett Butlers, and they are much cooler than the Ashley Wilkeses of the college campus—the guys who study hard, are considerate of their feelings, and listen to them. Those guys are a bit nerdy, good friendship material, but they don't take your breath away."[28]

The actions and the unrehearsed words of women reveal that they want something other than what they say they want. When women get the fair-minded, negotiating, household-chore-sharing men that feminists say they want, they mock them as "kitchen bitches" and divorce them, as Sandra Tsing Loh did in a piece of comically unrefined misandry she wrote for The Atlantic about her own decision to divorce. She mused about a bonobo solution to marriage wherein "the men/husbands/boyfriends come in once or twice a week to build shelves, prepare that bouillabaisse, or provide sex."[29] Hanna Rosin of "The End of Men" fame responded to the piece with a few confessions about her own husband, who she worried had usurped her in the kitchen by becoming a fine cook who enjoyed cooking for his family. Her feminist solution was to throw a cookbook across the room and "storm" upstairs. Now she rushes home from work to make dinner before her husband can, presumably, so she can feel more like a woman. And her husband, she said, simply "got the message" and "ceded some of the territory" back to her.[30]

As things have shaken out in the aftermath of the sexual revolution, men are better able to assert their interests in short-term relationships, and women are better able to assert their interests in long-term relationships. This is a familiar comic

---

28   Kimmel, Michael. *Guyland*. 2008. HarperCollins e-books. Loc. 4447. Kindle.

29   Tsing Loh, Sandra. "Let's Call the Whole Thing Off." *The Atlantic* July 2009. Web. 20 Mar. 2011. http://www.theatlantic.com/magazine/archive/2009/07/let-8217-s-call-the-whole-thing-off/7488/1/

30   Rosin, Hanna. "Rise of the Kitchen Bitch." *Slate*. N.p., 15 Dec. 2009. Web. 20 Mar. 2011. http://www.doublex.com/section/life/rise-kitchen-bitch

theme in film and television—men frustrate women by avoiding "commitment" (to a relationship) as long as they can, and women panic as their biological clocks tick and their viability in the sexual marketplace declines.

As young men, especially young men in disadvantaged socio-economic groups, have invested less effort in education and become less interested in pursuing the kinds of careers that lead to affluence in a global economy, and as the kinds of work many men enjoy has been degraded or exported to countries where labor is cheap, recycled calls to "reimagine masculinity" have become increasingly desperate.

Anti-rape and anti-violence activists like Jackson Katz have been talking for years about the "macho paradox"[31] and telling young men how it perpetuates violence against women.[32] The National Organization for Men Against Sexism (NOMAS) traces its roots to the 1970s. It counts "unlearning aggressiveness" and "un-learning large parts of the male role" among its basic tenets[33], and states in its principles[34] that "men can live as happier and more fulfilled human beings by challenging the old-fashioned rules of masculinity." "Reimagining masculinity" has also been a theme in the men's movement for some time.

As men struggled after the crash of the early 21st Century real estate boom with the insult of fewer construction jobs adding to the injury of outsourced manufacturing, previously ignored calls to address the "crisis in masculinity" were finally being heard by

---

31   Katz, Jackson. *The Macho Paradox : Why Some Men Hurt Women And How All Men Can Help*. 2006. Sourcebooks, Inc. Print.

32   Katz, Jackson. *Tough Guise : Violence, Media and the Crisis in Masculinity*. Media Education Foundation. 1999. Video.

33   "Tenets." nomas.org (National Organization for Men Against Sexism, official site). N.p., n.d. Web. 19 Mar. 2011. http://www.nomas.org/tenets

34   "Principles." nomas.org (National Organization for Men Against Sexism, official site). N.p., n.d. Web. 19 Mar. 2011. http://www.nomas.org/principles

a wider audience. In 2010, a Foundation for Male Studies[35] was formed in an attempt to create university programs to study the male condition. Its early promotional content seemed to echo concerns from both the men's rights and the pro-feminist communities that males are more likely to go to prison, commit suicide, or avoid seeking medical treatment. Many prominent men's rights activists, in agreement with the feminists they identify as enemies—as well as Bly and Keen before them—now believe that "masculinity has, as it relates to modern realities, corrupt, oppressive and destructive elements that need to change."[36] Some are positioning men as a new minority[37] group, a new social identity group asserting its interests by competing for a place at the grievance table alongside other sexual, ethnic, racial, and religious identity groups.

Feminists have no intention of allowing men to compete fairly with women as a grievance group, and some have turned their pleas for men to "reimagine masculinity" into an impatient command for men to "man up." Men are being told that they had better get out of their funk and abandon their "musty scripts" of masculinity in a hurry, because the globalist, feminist future isn't waiting for them any longer. Women are moving up, and if men need to do "girly jobs" to help women make ends meet or become stay-at-home dads to pick up a successful working mom's slack, then feminists say that's just how it's going to have to be. Men had better tie on their aprons and learn to like it.

The hypocrisy of feminists telling men to "man up" is that it invokes the same ancient masculine archetypes that all those

---

35   The Foundation for Male Studies. N.p., n.d. Web. 19 Mar. 2011. http://www.malestudies.org/index.html

36   Elam, Paul. "The Plague of Modern Masculinity." *A Voice for Men*. N.p., 17 July 2010. Web. 19 Mar. 2011. http://www.avoiceformen.com/2010/07/01/the-plague-of-modern-masculinity/

37   Ellison, Jesse. "Are Men The New Minority?" *Newsweek* 29 Sept. 2010. Web. 19 Mar. 2011. http://education.newsweek.com/2010/09/29/the-new-minority-on-campus-men.html

who have tried to "reimagine masculinity" have been trying to put to bed. They are ham-handedly trying to tap into the power of the very same "male culture" that they want to break down. They are telling men to prove their masculinity, after saying that men should no longer have to do that. They are selling men liberation from the "man code"[38] and then telling men how they must behave to be considered "good men."

In effect, feminists are now saying that a man must be strong, courageous, and even heroic in his willingness to sacrifice his own interests for the good of the tribe. From the mouths of feminists, this is crass and manipulative. Males may be faltering in educational achievement, but they're not dumb. Men in the past have made great sacrifices for honor and glory and the esteem of their male peers—not to mention rewards of booty and women. Feminists want men to shame and abandon the bold manhood of their forefathers for a pat on the head and the privilege of being called kitchen bitches.

The reimaginers of masculinity have failed to connect with mainstream men, and they are destined to fail so long as they refuse to deal with men as self-interested individuals. Their reimagined models of masculinity will fail to inspire the majority of men so long as they actively reject the natural primacy of strength in the male hierarchy of virtues.

Osama bin Laden famously remarked that "when people see a strong horse and a weak horse, by nature, they will like the strong horse."[39]

All of these "reimagined masculinities" are weak horses.

38   Schwyzer, Hugo. "How Men's Rights Activists Get Feminism Wrong." *The Good Men Project.* N.p., 8 Mar. 2011. Web. 19 Mar. 2011. http://goodmenproject.com/ethics-values/how-the-mens-rights-activists-get-feminism-wrong

39   "Transcript of Osama bin Laden videotape." *CNN.com.* CNN, 13 Dec. 2001. Web. 19 Mar. 2011. http://articles.cnn.com/2001-12-13/us/tape.transcript_1_bin-shaykh-al-bahrani-diplomatic-language-services?_s=PM:US

Calling yourself a wild man does not make you wild, and everyone knows it.

Pacifist "fierce gentlemen" and "democratic men" are restricted to talking tough—they can say whatever they want because they don't have to back it up. Tough talkers and civilized blowhards of both sexes can speak their minds with impunity only in a lawful society secured by the threat of violence from armed men (and women). If manliness can be reduced to "assertiveness," as Harvey Mansfield asserted, then he was right to say that Margaret Thatcher was a manly woman.[40]

If "manning up" means taking whatever job you can get to support your family or changing diapers or doing whatever women want you to do, why call it "manning up" at all? Why not just call it "being responsible" or "being obedient?" Writer Amada Hess was correct when she observed that Doupkil and Romano's calls to "reimagine masculinity" merely re-codified masculinity as "personhood."[41]

Reimagining masculinity is a self-esteem-building project for impotent men, and an impotence-building project for men with self-esteem.

To maintain any kind of civilization, men have to give up a certain amount of their personal sovereignty. The Romans used the fasces as a symbol of the collected power of men—a bundle of rods strapped to an axe, wielded by the state. Men agree to surrender some autonomy to the state for the promise of security and order. The state provides a means for men to resolve their disputes and replaces the nasty, brutish, and unpredictable

40   Mansfield, Harvey C. *Manliness*. 2006. Yale University Press.

41   Hess, Amanda. "Newsweek's "the new macho": It's the new "person"!" TBD. 21 Sept. 2010. Web. 20 Mar. 2011. http://www.tbd.com/blogs/amanda-hess/2010/09/newsweek-s-the-new-macho-it-s-the-new-person-2051.html

violence of total chaos with an orderly dispensation of collective violence. The state becomes the axe.

However, as the state grows, it requires ever greater sacrifices of personal power to maintain order. Men make these sacrifices reluctantly until, over time, the state gains enough power to demand and do whatever it wants, with or without the majority mandate of men. Today, our leaders openly mock men who are unwilling to give the state complete control over life and death.[42]

The desire to reimagine masculinity is a symptom of enslavement. Men have given virtually all of their power to the state. Many European countries have disarmed their citizens, and men are at the mercy of states that claim to act in their collective best interests. Even a century ago, men gathered in the streets to violently overthrow corrupt governments. Today, most Americans couldn't conceive of doing more than holding a candlelight vigil. Many western men have given up sole proprietorships and crafts and other activities that offer the satisfaction of willed agency and traded this kind of fulfillment for comfortable but unfulfilling busywork jobs at large corporations where men are merely ants and women make perkier workers. As women gain political and financial influence, men are giving up their sovereignty at home, becoming mere peasants to capricious, emasculating queens who can call upon the axe of the state the moment they feel challenged or threatened. A mere whisper from a woman can place a man in shackles and force him to either confess or prove that he is innocent of even the pettiest charges.

Feminists and socialists are content to entrust the state with their care, protection, and employment. Chafetz admitted that make-work jobs would have to be created to facilitate her

---

42   Kuhnhenn, Jim. "Obama says some voters are angry, bitter." *USA Today* (Associated Press). 12 April 2008. Web. 26 Mar. 2011. http://www.usatoday.com/news/topstories/2008-04-11-3235435230_x.htm

gender-neutral utopia, and she fantasized about a world without the guns that "many American males cling to" as an "expression of their virility."[43]

The reimaginers of masculinity have realized, perhaps subconsciously, that men still want to feel like men. To humor men and better acclimate them to a captive, powerless existence, the reimaginers have taken it upon themselves to decorate the cage a bit. They have attempted to provide safe narratives that offer men the feel of expressing a virtual virility without the danger it poses to the interests of women and the status quo. They have brainstormed for ways to empower men without actually giving them any real power. To pacify man, they offered him only the "mother-may-I" masculinities most compatible with the interests of women.

It is truly profound that, when the reimaginers of masculinity prepared to sell their domesticated manhoods to everyday man, even they could not imagine a way to appeal to him without resorting to coercive testing language of the male groups, the primal vocabulary of violence, or by appealing to his desire to demonstrate strength, courage, mastery and a sense of honor.

---

43   Saltzman Chaftez, Janet. *Masculine, Feminine or Human?* 2nd ed. Itasca: Peacock Publishers, 1978. 257. Print.

Part 3 – "Misrepresenting Masculinity"

THE FORTY-NINE PERCENT MAJORITY

Over the last few decades, many have attempted to "reimagine" masculinity. People realized that despite the calls of feminists to abandon concepts of gender altogether, and despite—as we will see—the firmly held belief among social scientists that sex roles were merely learned social scripts, men and women still maintained separate social identities. Men were particularly concerned with being perceived by others as being manly or masculine, and with avoiding the emasculating stigma of effeminacy. Women and male feminists continue to find this confounding. Upon finishing a series of studies that connected displays of aggression to maintaining masculine identity, researcher Jennifer K. Bosson recently admitted to *Time* magazine:

> "When I was younger I felt annoyed by my male friends who would refuse to hold a pocketbook or say whether they thought another man was attractive. I thought it was a personal shortcoming that they were so anxious about their manhood. Now I feel much more sympathy for men..."[1]

The article, written by a woman, was condescendingly titled "Masculinity, a Delicate Flower." The researcher said men were "anxious" and the findings indicated that men were more likely to engage in displays of aggression when their status as men was "threatened." This is characteristic of the way that masculinity is pathologized in the modern media. Concern about masculine status and identity—what I would call honor—is presented as a curious male "hang up" that impedes their progress in the march to postmodern utopian feminist bliss. When men assert themselves, when they defend their honor, when they "man

---

1   Melnick, Meredith. "Masculinity, a Delicate Flower." *Time* 5 May 2011. Web. 24 May 2011.

up" and demonstrate strength, courage and mastery—they are portrayed as being insecure fakes who are fearful, desperate and weak.

If men are weak and insecure, then, compared to what standard? Compared to women, who spend billions each year on cosmetics, fashion, weight loss gimmicks, plastic surgery, self-help books, psychotherapy, anti-depressants, and the mail order spirituality of grifting gurus from Benny Hinn to Deepak Chopra and Oprah Winfrey?

This has been going on for a long time. This kind of biased positioning is evident in the majority of articles, books and textbooks dealing with masculinity. John Wayne died in 1979, and two of the iconic Marlboro men died of cancer in the early 1990s, but these cliché feminist bêtes noires are still burned in effigy in virtually every mainstream anti-masculinity op-ed.

To better understand The Way of Men, it is important to understand how men and masculinity have been caricatured and misrepresented by those with an ideological agenda. To grasp how feminists have misunderstood men, it is helpful to understand their perception of men. Where do their ideas about traditional manhood come from? What are their working assumptions about masculinity, femininity, and sex roles? It is also useful to be able to separate thoughtful writing about masculinity from so many thoughtless refrains.

In his 1976 book *The Forty-Nine Percent Majority*, behavioral psychologist and NOMAS co-founder[2] Robert Brannon pieced together a folksy model of American manhood for the sole purpose of taking it apart. Brannon claimed that the male sex role in 20th Century American society had four dimensions, or basic themes.

2   "Leadership." nomas.org (National Organization for Men Against Sexism, official site). Web. 23 Apr. 2011. http://www.nomas.org/leadership

No Sissy Stuff: The stigma of all stereotyped feminine characteristics and qualities, including openness and vulnerability.

The Big Wheel: Success, status, and the need to be looked up to.

The Sturdy Oak: A manly air of toughness, confidence and self-reliance.

Give 'Em Hell!: The aura of aggression, violence and daring.[3]

The Forty-Nine Percent Majority is out of print, but Brannon's list remains influential. Michael Kimmel, who is considered by many to be the leading expert in men's studies, has reprinted or referred reverently to Brannon's list in most of the books he has written on the study of gender. Kimmel's 2009 book, *Guyland*, also included the list. Brannon's four dimensions of the male sex role have been discussed in a wide range of recent books, textbooks, and articles on rape, sports, transsexuality, psychotherapy, homosexuality, education, fatherhood, bullying, Alzheimer's, nursing, race, and Christian living.[4] While comparatively few people have read the book, Brannon's "no sissy stuff" list continues to shape both popular and academic ideas about masculinity. Once you've read Brannon's introductory essay and flipped through *The Forty-Nine Percent Majority*, every argument, every "controversial" headline and every "new" study about masculinity coming from the profeminist camp will read like recycled boilerplate from the age of polyester bellbottoms and pet rocks. It's one of the ur-texts of profeminist mens' studies.

The Forty-Nine Percent Majority was a collection of essays edited by both Brannon and sociologist Deborah S. David. The book's

---

3   David, Deborah S., and Robert Brannon, eds. *The Forty-Nine Percent Majority : The Male Sex Role*. Philippines: Addison-Wesley Publishing Company, 1976. 1-42. Print.

4   A quick Google Books search for "Brannon Big Wheel Sissy" yielded over 200 references to Brannon's list in various books and journals for popular as well as academic audiences.

introductory essay in which the "no sissy stuff" list appears was titled, "The Male Sex Role: Our Culture's Blueprint of Manhood, and What it's Done for Us Lately." Brannon and David wrote that, in attempting to define the male sex role, they were "essentially defining a new area of study." [5] Brannon is normally credited with the "Blueprint" essay, and it is partially autobiographical, so I will refer to him alone as its author for the sake of brevity. Other contributors to *The Forty-Nine Percent Majority* included feminists Warren Farrell (*The Myth of Male Power*), Kate Millet (*Sexual Politics, The Prostitution Papers*), Lucy Komisar, Marc Feigen Fasteau (*The Male Machine*), and Jack Sawyer (*On Male Liberation*).

Brannon began with the concept of the social role as it pertained to the theatre. The role comes from the French, meaning the roll of paper an actor's part is written on. He offered the role of Hamlet as an example. Brannon then defined the social role as "any pattern of behaviors which a given individual in a specified (set of) situation(s) is both: (1) expected and (2) encouraged and/ or trained to perform."[6] A role is distinguished from a stereotype, because an individual may or may not be encouraged or expected to live up to a stereotype.

Brannon stated that he and "other young social scientists" at the time believed that the "most promising answer to most questions about human behavior" would not be found by studying ancient history or biology, but by studying the "invisible but almost irresistible social patterns of pressure which shape and direct the behavior of every man and every woman."[7] Though Brannon didn't deal with the nurture vs. nature dilemma explicitly, his emphasis on role learning places him deep in the nurture camp with anthropologist Margaret Mead. In fact, Brannon rested

---

5   David, Deborah S., and Robert Brannon, eds. *The Forty-Nine Percent Majority : The Male Sex Role*. Philippines: Addison-Wesley Publishing Company, 1976. vii. Print.

6   Ibid. 5.

7   Ibid. 3.

his "Blueprint" argument concerning the importance of learned roles in determining sex-differentiated behavior on Mead's study of three primitive societies in New Guinea: the Arapesh, the Mundugumor, and the Tchambuli. Mead's characterizations of sex roles in these societies, it was later revealed, were either flawed or flat-out wrong.

According to Brannon's reading of Mead, both male and female members of the Arapesh tended to be "passive, cooperative and peaceful," and their culture tended toward feminine behavior as a whole. Brannon failed to note that Reo Fortune, who was married to Mead and who studied the Arapesh with her in New Guinea, characterized the Arapesh quite differently. In his 1939 article "Arapesh Warfare," Fortune explained that although a great deal of war-making had been suppressed by German occupation of their land, the Arapesh maintained a long tradition of wife stealing. This tended to be the major aim of their violent conflicts. The old men of the tribe bragged about their war kills from more violent times, and if they had none, they bragged about their hunting records. Fortune rejected Mead's claim that the Arapesh expected and exhibited similar temperaments in the sexes. Arapesh men even seemed to maintain, as men often do, a hierarchy of masculinity within their clans. Fortune wrote:

> "...we may cite the proverb, aramumip ulukwip nahaiya; aramagowep ulukwip nahaiya, "Men's hearts are different; women's hearts are different," and also the existence of a class of men called aramagowem, "women male," or effeminate men. The class of aramagowem is a definitely assigned class, with definite functions, given inferior food at feasts and special subordinate place. The man, Djeguh, mentioned in our accounts of faction feud and of war, was, for example, an aramatokwin, "woman male" (the singular form of aramago-wem). He was never suspected of cowardice in war. He was, however, without ability in men's dances, oratory, economic leadership, and in his understanding. He was found by the

writer to be very reticent and quiet."[8]

Mead also explained away the swaggering, bossy alphas of the villages—the "big men"—as self-sacrificing fellows who, though they weren't really predisposed to that sort of assertiveness, had to pretend to be "big men" for the sake of the community. In 2003, having visited Arapesh country himself, anthropologist Paul Roscoe reviewed the work of Mead and Fortune. He wrote that Mead "got it wrong," and that Fortune, "more accurately depicted Mountain Arapesh warfare."[9] Early reviewers noted that several details of Mead's own account of the Arapesh seem to invalidate her colored conclusion that they were a peaceful people, and several other anthropologists have agreed that Mead portrayed the Arapesh inaccurately. [10]

Both the men and women of a neighboring tribe, the Mundugumor, are described by Brannon (via Mead) as being aggressive and belligerent. There is nothing particularly noteworthy about finding a tribe of warlike people. The relevant point here is that the males and females of the tribe were portrayed as being equally aggressive. One would have to maintain a naïve and sheltered sense of things to imagine that women are non-violent by nature. Indeed, YouTube and reality television frequently provide us with examples of females behaving barbarously. We don't have to fly to New Guinea to observe violent women. Females are clearly capable of aggression. Were both the male and female members of the Mundugumor tribe equally aggressive? Given all of the other data available about humans and other apes, as well as Mead's tendency to see things as she wanted to see them, it's

8   Fortune, R.F. "Arapesh Warfare." *American Anthropologist* 1.1 Jan. (1939): 22-41. JSTOR. Web. 25 Apr. 2011. http://www.jstor.org/stable/661720

9   Roscoe, Paul. "Margaret Mead, Reo Fortune, and Mountain Arapesh Warfare." *American Anthropologist* 105.31 Sept. (2003): 581-91. JSTOR. Web. 26 Apr. 2011. http://www.jstor.org/stable/3566907

10   Bashkow, Ira, and Lise M. Dobrin. "The Anthropologist's Fieldwork as Lived World: Margaret Mead and Reo Fortune among the Mountain Arapesh." *Paideuma* 53 (2007): 79-87. JSTOR. Web. 27 Apr. 2011. http://www.jstor.org/stable/40341946

easy to write her assertion off as more subjective interpretation.

To support his theory that culturally determined sex roles are primarily responsible for the differences in behavior between human males and females, Brannon cites Mead's research on the Tchambuli people. Tchambuli males are described as being "sensitive, artisitic, gossipy, fond of adornment and emotionally dependent." According to Brannon and Mead, Tchambuli females were expected to be "competent, dominating, practical and efficient," as well as being sexually aggressive. Deborah Gewertz did some fieldwork with the Tchambuli, or Chambri (as she referred to them) in 1974 and 1975. She noted in a 1981 paper on the subject that the "(in the literature of women's studies) Chambri women had achieved the status of icons because of their significant and dominant roles within their villages." Her own perception of gender relations among the Chambri was somewhat different from what Mead saw years earlier, and she suspected that what Mead had witnessed was a reduced level of competition between Chambri men due to temporary economic and historical influences. When Mead was observing them, the Chambri men had recently lost a war, and the tribe was in exile. The Chambri women ended up doing a lot of fishing, and therefore, temporarily wielded more economic influence. The men were biding their time and looking for ways to re-establish dominance in the region. It was through the fishing efforts of the women that the men were able to re-establish their status among the neighboring tribes.[11]

Gewertz's assessment is particularly interesting in light of the shifts of economic power that are happening between men and women in the United States. Men and women are not interchangeable, and their social roles are not the only meaningful causes of their differing behaviors, but they can

---

11　　　　Gewertz, Deborah. "A Historical Reconsideration of Female Dominance among the Chambri of Papua New Guinea." *American Ethnologist*, 8.11 Feb. (1981): 94-106. JSTOR. Web. 27 Apr. 2011. http://www.jstor.org/stable/644489

occasionally swap duties to help each other through tough or uncertain times. A few years ago, I worked a delivery job with a strapping, competent fellow who eventually decided to stay home with his children because his wife was making a lot of money as a nurse while his wages were barely covering day care costs. It made more sense for him to stay home, and his kids were almost certainly better off for having their father around. He was not an effeminate man by any measure, but one wonders what fanciful assertions Mead or Brannon might have made about the flexibility of sex roles had they studied his family.

As Gewertz alluded, by the 1970s, Mead's research had become extremely popular in feminist circles for what it seemed to imply about human nature and the relationship between the sexes. Based on her interpretation of Arapesh, the Mundugumor and the Tchambuli cultures, Mead famously concluded in 1935 that:

> "many, if not all, of the personality traits which we have called masculine or feminine are as lightly linked to sex as are the clothing, the manners, and the form of head-dress that a society at a given period assigns to either sex."[12]

Mead made sex roles appear to be as superficial and arbitrary as fashion, and one can easily imagine the influence that might have had on budding feminist ideologues like Brannon. As we have seen above, however, Mead's depictions of the tribes that led her to draw these kinds of conclusions could charitably be described as "incomplete." As this is the stated basis for Brannon's belief that sex roles are almost wholly learned—and can therefore be unlearned or re-shaped completely—his conception of the male sex role is left standing on extremely shaky ground. As more people study the societies that Mead wrote about, the sex-role patterns within those groups have become increasingly familiar.

---

12   Margaret, Mead. Sex and Temperament: In Three Primitive Societies. 1935. Harper Perennial, 2001. 262. Print.

According to Derek Freeman, Mead's most notorious and persistent critic, Margaret Mead's questionable research played a pivotal part in shifting the anthropological zeitgeist in the early 20th Century from biological determinism to cultural determinism. In the late 19th Century, the work of Charles Darwin appeared to validate long-held and somewhat reasonable suspicions about the importance of heredity in determining human behavior. Man had long bred animals and been aware that animals had certain temperaments and physical characteristics that could be passed on to the next generation. Groups of humans seemed to have heritable physical and behavioral characteristics, too, so it was not a great stretch to imagine that the future of a human population could be controlled by aiding the process of natural selection through selective breeding.

The study of eugenics[13]—"the self direction of human evolution"—became popular and eugenic laws were passed in both Europe and the United States. Sir Francis Galton, the father of eugenics, had declared in 1873 that, "when nature and nurture compete for supremacy on equal terms," nature is always proven stronger.[14] Evolutionary biologists Richard Wrangham and Dale Peterson referred to Galton's framing of the enduring "nature vs. nurture" debate as "Galton's Error" because the forces of nature and nurture are always interacting in humans.[15]

It was during the height of the heated nature vs. nurture debate, however, that Margaret Mead came of age. According to Freeman, Mead's mentor Franz Boas was searching for convincing evidence to substantiate his belief that "social stimulus" had a far greater influence over human behavior than "the biological mechanism." When Mead went to Samoa at the age of 23 to study

13   Fun fact: εὐγενής, the Greek root of eugenics means well-born, of noble race, of high descent. It is also the root of the name "Eugene."

14   Freeman, Derek. *Margaret Mead and Samoa*. N.p.: Harvard University Press, 1983. 10. Print.

15   Wrangham, Richard, and Dale Peterson. *Demonic Males : Apes and the Origins of Human Violence*. New York: Mariner Books/Houghton Mifflin Company, 1996. 95. Print.

adolescence there, she was looking for a "negative instance"—a conflicting account that disproved a long held generalization about human behavior. In this case, the long held generalization she hoped to disprove by offering a single exception was the belief that adolescence was a difficult period. Seeking this negative instance, Mead published a gloss of Samoan society that downplayed sources of tension and conflict and portrayed the Samoan lifestyle as one characterized by relative ease.[16] Her example of Samoa was lauded by Boas, immediately became a bestseller, and has since become a favorite of advocates for sexual freedom and feminism the world over. Moreover, the influence of her research and its emphasis on negative instances that seemed to prove the importance of nurture over nature is evident in Brannon's "Blueprint" essay.

Freeman noted that Mead was "denied entry to all chiefly fonos" because she was a woman and "had no participation in the political life of Ta'aū." She lived with a Western host family in a Western home, and conducted the majority of her research by interviewing little girls.[17] Freeman, citing his own first hand observations of Samoan political life and the observations of many men who had visited the island over the preceding century, characterized the Samoans as competitive, jealous, prideful and obsessed with rank. Strangely, Mead had portrayed the Samoans as a peaceful, causal people who had no war gods, who didn't esteem bravery, and who didn't give a special place in society to the warrior. Fully half of the pagan Samoan gods were in fact war gods, and the Samoans had a long history of slaughtering—possibly even cannibalizing—a huge percentage of their rivals. Samoan men believed it was a great honor to die in battle. Political power was given to those who had conquered or shown bravery in battle. When Freeman repeated Mead's quotes about

---

16   Freeman, Derek. *Margaret Mead and Samoa*. N.p.: Harvard University Press, 1983. 82-94. Print.

17   Ibid. 66-73, 131. Ta'aū, the largest island in American Samoa, was the island she famously studied.

warriors holding no place of importance in Samoan society to a high ranking Samoan man, he became irate.[18]

The flaws in Mead's research had not been fully revealed at the time Brannon wrote *The Forty-Nine Percent Majority*. However, like Mead, Brannon's theories relied on wishful thinking. Mead's research was embraced because it told certain people—people like Brannon—what they wanted to hear about human nature and gender. Brannon's depiction of the male sex role and the idea that its script can be re-written completely builds on Mead's wishful thinking, and appeals to feminists because it is essential to their concept of a gender-neutral society.

The hard biological determinism of Galton overshot reality and was used to justify eugenics laws that were sometimes unnecessarily cruel, or based on faulty assumptions. The emphasis on hard cultural determinism advanced by Mead, Boas and Brannon nurtures another sort of hubris, and is employed by enthusiastic social engineers to justify their quack programs and policies. The traditional approach has been to recognize human nature as prone to wickedness and craft social solutions that curb or redirect the aspects of our natures that make civilized living impossible. Humans are social animals, and the human way has always been to seek a balance between nature and nurture.

Do male sex roles exist?

Of course they do.

Do the particulars of the male sex role vary from culture to culture, due to differences in economics, religion, resources, technological advancement, weather, historical factors and innumerable cultural idiosyncrasies and influences?

---

18   Ibid. 157-173.

Of course they do.

However, Mead and Brannon rejected the importance of biological influences in shaping those roles. Culturally determined sex roles undoubtedly influence the way men and women conduct themselves. Brannon's error—and the error of his many ideological heirs who would attempt, again and again, to "reimagine" masculinity—was in portraying social sex roles as all-important. All cultures have different "scripts" for the sexes, but the scripts can't simply be re-written from scratch. To borrow an example from Brannon's essay, many actors have played and interpreted the role of Hamlet. The role has been re-written and adapted and many different versions have been produced. But you can only fool around with it so much—something of significance has to remain of the original character for us to recognize the similarity. After a certain number of deviations, the character is no longer Hamlet.

Attempts to understand masculinity present a "Ship of Theseus" paradox. Thesus' ship was preserved as a monument by the Athenians for many years, and according to Plutarch's account, the Athenians had replaced the old planks as they decayed with new and stronger timber. He remarked that "this ship became a standing example among the philosophers, for the logical question of things that grow; one side holding that the ship remained the same, and the other contending that it was not the same."

Will any script do, so long as it is assigned to biological males and carefully taught to them? If not, how many parts can be replaced or exchanged before what we recognize as masculinity is no longer recognizable? Can a sturdy beam be replaced with a rotten plank?

Most anthropologists are quick to acknowledge the historical importance of Mead's pioneering work and her contributions to the field of anthropology, but it is clear that she did not succeed in finding a "negative instance" with regard to sex roles. No one else has, either. Donald Brown's list of Human Universals [19]identifies the following as norms for males:

Cross-Cultural Norms for Males in Human Societies[20]

- Male and female and adult and child seen as having different natures.
- Males dominate public/political realm.
- Males engage in more coalitional violence.
- Males more aggressive.
- Males more prone to lethal violence.
- Males more prone to theft.
- Males, on average, travel greater distances over lifetime.

Is it simply due to an arbitrarily determined sex-role—a script that can be re-written from scratch—that people all over the world share some of the same basic ideas about men?

Before we review the content of Brannon's list itself, there's another list I came across that puts many discussions about sex roles and masculinity in perspective. It could be considered "the one list to rule them all" because it isn't locked in one time or place or culture. It is neither a "wish list" detailing how someone thinks men should behave, nor a diagnosis. Evolutionary biologist Randy Thornhill and cultural anthropologist Craig T. Palmer came up with a list of predictions, based on evolutionary theory, for male mammals "with a history of greater sexual selection on males than females."[21]

---

19   Brown, Donald E. "Human Universals." DePaul University, n.d. Web. 19 Feb. 2011. http://condor.depaul.edu/mfiddler/hyphen/humunivers.htm

20   Ibid.

21   Thornhill, Randy and Palmer, Craig T., *A Natural History of Rape : Biological Bases of Sexual Coercion*. The MIT Press. 2000. 37-38. Print.

Comparative Predictions for Male Mammals, in Species Where Sexual Selection is Greater on Males[22]

- Males will be larger than females.
- More males than females will be conceived and born.
- Males will die younger as a result of physiological malfunction than females.
- Males will engage in more risky activities in the context of acquiring mates than females.
- Males will have higher mortality than females as a result of external causes, such as combat, disease, and accidents.
- Males will exhibit more general aggression than females.
- More often than females, males will engage in escalating violent aggression that leads to injury and even death.
- Pre-adult males will engage in more competitive and aggressive play than pre-adult females.
- Males will be less discriminating about and more eager to copulate with females than vice-versa.

As mentioned earlier in this book, evolutionary theory predicts that because the parental effort required of human females is much greater than that of human males, there will be more competition between human males to access that effort, and males will be selected in part for their ability to overcome other males in competition for mating opportunities. For humans living in complex societies, the process of selection is far more complicated than simply having the strength and courage necessary to overcome one's enemies in hand-to-hand combat or achieve a higher status within a group hierarchy, but for most of human evolutionary history, fortune—and females—favored the strong and the bold.

Now, let's take another look at Brannon's list.

---

22   Ibid. Note: Thornhill and Palmer's list was a collection of predictions made wide variety of scientists, who were cited in their original lists. Readers are highly encouraged to purchase Thornhill and Palmer's book, and investigate those references themselves. MIT Press is encouraged to get with it and make this excellent book available via Kindle, iPad, etc.

Three out of four of his hokey slogans contain advice that is, from an evolutionary perspective, quite sound and in line with the predictions listed above.

The Big Wheel: Success, status, and the need to be looked up to.

The Sturdy Oak: A manly air of toughness, confidence and self-reliance.

Give 'Em Hell!: The aura of aggression, violence and daring.

Brannon presented these themes as part of an arbitrary script, a role society encourages males to play, a false front that men must fake in order to "make it." One of Brannon's intellectual descendants, pro-feminist anti-rape activist Jackson Katz, has referred to this as a "tough guise" and has made a career for himself out of blaming the media for promoting images of violent masculinity. From an evolutionary standpoint, Brannon's slogans are simply folk renditions of solid advice for males who want to win the evolutionary game. In straightforward terms, Brannon's big wheel, sturdy oak, and "give 'em hell" themes are messages telling men to signal high status within the male group, and to demonstrate strength, courage, and competence.

No Sissy Stuff: The stigma of all stereotyped feminine characteristics and qualities, including openness and vulnerability.

Brandon listed "No Sissy Stuff," as the first dimension of the male sex role. He correctly noted that while females will naturally identify with their mothers, because they are both the same sex, at some point, males will look to male role models to shape their identities. Then he gave several examples of how men and women alike scold boys when they behave like girls, and how men will go out of their way to avoid being seen as effeminate. He employed the standard tactic of taking a fairly innocuous practice that was culturally assigned to women, and then making men look neurotic for wanting nothing to do with something so harmless. One example was a 230-pound linebacker who was asked if he was worried about looking like a "sissy" because he did needlepoint in his spare time. In a cheap, classic reductio ad Hitlerum, Brannon then provided a quote by Adolf Hitler, explaining why he didn't want a wife who was overly intelligent. The insinuation, of course, was that any man who was concerned with his own reputation as a man—with masculine honor—was morally aligned with Adolf Hitler.[23]

It is true, as Ms. Bosson above "discovered," that men sometimes avoid activities that seem trivial, simply because they are associated with women or effeminate men. Pointing this out is an easy way to make men and masculinity appear to be absurd or ridiculous. When doing things that are out of sync with the male sex role, men today often joke that they are "secure about their masculinity," so they aren't worried about it. Ironically, this is usually a strategy men employ to diffuse criticism and one-up each other. It is a form of bragging that says, "I have so much excess credibility as a man that I don't need to concern myself with petty infractions of man code." The need to acknowledge the infraction is an acknowledgement of the code, and an indication that the man in question is, in fact, at least slightly uncomfortable with breaking it. Saying that you are unconcerned with breaking codes of masculinity is an indirect way to challenge male peers and make yourself seem ballsy and invincible, while making others seem fearful and vulnerable.

Cultural codes of masculinity can be idiosyncratic, because they accumulate references and associations over long periods of time—and it is not uncommon for men to avoid behaviors or activities without really knowing why. For instance, there is nothing particularly male or female about doing the dishes.

---

23   David, Deborah S., and Robert Brannon, eds. *The Forty-Nine Percent Majority : The Male Sex Role*. Philippines: Addison-Wesley Publishing Company, 1976. 16. Print.

Men engaged in the manliest, riskiest, all-male activities—on whaling ships, in the military, on the frontier—have washed their own cups and plates. However, in married households, women have traditionally ended up with that bit of labor, so there is a lingering cultural association that regards doing the dishes as "women's work." This is a bit silly, and most men recognize that, but few men would brag that they always do the dishes—at least to their male friends.

Brannon complained that men avoid emotional openness and vulnerability, but he failed to acknowledge or even consider the obvious tactical advantages of being choosy about with whom one shares his tears. In *The Forty-Nine Percent Majority*, Warren Farrell (who later wrote *The Myth of Male Power*) elaborated on the theme. He characterized the men of his time as being "emotionally incompetent" and "emotionally constipated," and associated the male resistance to crying in public with passive resistance to black integration among whites. Farrell wrote that men create a "masculine mystique" by hiding their emotions, and theorized that we would be better policed and governed if our male leaders cried and admitted their failure openly. He naively—almost childishly—wondered why people would question a man's ability to lead other men, or a nation, if he appeared to be emotionally vulnerable.[24] In the essay that followed, Jack O. Balswick and Charles W. Peek melodramatically referred to the "inexpressive male" as a "tragedy of American society," but failed to articulate why the confident stoicism of the John Wayne cowboy or the James Bond (isn't Bond British?) playboy was so "tragic."[25]

Like so many male feminists, the male writers that David and Brannon chose to feature in *The Forty-Nine Percent Majority* repeated the sentiments of women without thinking critically

---

24   Ibid. "The Politics of Vulnerability." 51-54.

25   Ibid. "The Inexpressive Male: A Tragedy of American Society." 55-57.

about why men behave the way they do. If women were "free" to cry in public, so the logic goes, men would be "freer" if they cried in public, too. The word "vulnerability" has acquired a certain cachet in the gynocentric worlds of feminist thought, but to most men, it remains what it has always been—a technical euphemism for weakness. Exposing a "vulnerability," to men, is like rolling over and offering your belly to anyone who would take it. It's not a positive. It's something you would do only around someone whom you trust completely. Women have a habit of throwing men's exposed emotional vulnerabilities back at them in heated arguments, and many men have been burned for baring their souls. Even in the context of a private relationship, many men have good reasons to avoid showing women or men the things that really get to them.

If you look at vulnerability from the perspective of a group hierarchy, it becomes obvious why men don't want to expose their vulnerabilities publicly, and why men distance themselves from men who are obviously vulnerable. Crying is perfectly natural. It's a perfectly natural admission of defeat, emotional exhaustion, fear, or powerlessness. A man who is "vulnerable" is a weak link. He's shown that he is going to break under pressure, or that he is prone to manipulation. Tactically, this is a problem for the group, and as a result, he is going to lose status within the group. Men who appear to be unflappable, however, make the group look watertight. It makes perfect sense for men to want to ally themselves with strong men who can pull their weight, and who don't dishonor the group. From a primal perspective, dishonor is danger. It should be obvious why a group of men competing with other groups of men for survival would want to appear to be strong, courageous, and competent.

All of this primal posturing may seem absurd, say, in an office or walking around the mall, but status still matters. While the popular media sometimes paints a feminist fantasy of what its most privileged, successful women want from men (usually it still comes down to resources and ego stroking) men on the ground observe women selecting for high status or the appearance of high status all the time.[26] Just as many young girls strive to be in and exclude each other from the most popular cliques, it makes sense for men to increase their status by courting high status groups of men. Even the lowest status male in a group of high status males stands a better chance of snagging a decent piece of tail than he might on his own, but the mating game is only part of the equation. Membership in a high-status group confers many benefits, including access to desirable social networks, resources, and protection from harassment.

Sound a little high-schoolish? Perhaps. Most would agree, however, that a good way to become more successful is to surround oneself with successful people.

Avoiding "sissy stuff" is not merely about a desire to differentiate oneself from one's mother and find a separate identity among men—although it is certainly that, too. "No Sissy Stuff" is an admonition to young men that routes them away from apparently submissive behaviors and influences and interests that could handicap them—and could make them appear vulnerable—as they compete and socialize with other men. If you're theoretically trying to be selected by a woman, as a man, why would you want to run the risk of being mistaken for a woman, instead of trying to prove that you're among the best men? Why wouldn't you advertise yourself as an exemplary man?

When throwing around evolutionary jargon, it is important to remember that as humans evolved, they were unaware of evolutionary processes. Even now that we are aware of evolutionary theory, we do not consciously play evolution's game. Sexual selection simply shaped our bodies and our drives to give

---

26   Some of the best non-mainstream media writing about the way sexual selection plays out in real life can be found at http://roissy.wordpress.com/ 2021 NOTE: This blog is gone, but eventually became https://heartiste.org, which still exists as an archive as of this writing, but has not been active since 2019.

us tactical advantages in the primal environment. Technology and the complexity of our civilization have fouled up a lot of the variables, even as our monkey brains remain essentially the same.

For instance, my best pal is a strategic and mechanical thinker with average to above-average intelligence. He is a natural fighter—large, quick, strong, and athletic. He doesn't have to put on a show to exude an aura of confidence, toughness, aggression, violence, or daring. In fact, he has to make a conscious effort to dial all of those qualities back just to function in polite society. Most men simply allow him to dominate a conversation, even if he clearly has no idea what he is talking about. He has all of the hunter traits, to the extent that even at the age of thirty, he can barely sit still and needs to be actively engaged in some kind of challenging task to avoid slipping into a minor, restless depression.

My friend has absolutely no "game." Healthy, attractive females ask for his number and send him provocative, semi-nude pictures of themselves directly to his phone. I've seen it happen over and over. I've seen the photos and the desperate text messages. All he has to do is show up at a bar, relax and let nature take its course. In a primal environment, in the absence of birth control, he'd have a sizeable brood of mini-monsters. Ironically, because he can have the pick of the most attractive females, he often ends up dating strippers on birth control who have large breast implants. Their technologically enhanced mammaries probably fool his primal brain into thinking they are ideal for suckling his offspring. Evolution's game—which he is designed to win—keeps leading his genes to a false victory, and an evolutionary dead end. Due to the dysgenic quirks of our very new, modern world, he is a natural alpha who is being selected out of the gene pool. I've often joked with him that, as far as evolution is concerned, he is being trounced by a weak, sickly Mormon accountant raising eight kids somewhere in Utah.

The point here is not to say that we need to realign our society to match primal circumstances in every way, or institute some sort of eugenics program. It is simply to say that the male sex role, roughly as Brannon describes it, endures because it is consistent with the way our species evolved, and the idea that we can simply rewrite the script from scratch or re-imagine the male sex role completely to suit the preferences of fashionable ideologies is absurd. The apparent de-motivation of men in contemporary society is a direct result of attempts to ignore history and evolution and re-imagine manhood in a way that is inconsistent with human nature.

I've written that Brannon pieced together his folksy model of manhood for the sole purpose of taking it apart. Brannon was not trying to understand men so much as he was trying to change them. I have made a point throughout to characterize his list as "folksy" and "hokey" because I think building the book *The Forty-Nine Percent Majority* around a collection of dated, goofy slogans was intentional or at least convenient to his aims. Instead of trying to understand why men behave the way they do, or investigate why men in most cultures[27] seem to revere strength, courage, competence, and high group status, Brannon caricatured manly virtues, failed to entertain the benefits of aspirational masculinity, focused on the losers in male hierarchical struggles and portrayed men as clueless marionettes who were simply being manipulated by an out-dated script.

> "...like the insecure politicians who decided to "hang tough" in Vietnam, like the ulcer-driven executives in their paneled offices, like the strutting youth-gang leaders, the young G.I.'s at My Lai, the ambitious counter-culture gurus, the casual and unfeeling rapists, and the silent Walter Mitty's who only dream...we each have been dancing the crippling steps, are

---

27   Even in Brannon's time, it was known that the majority of cultures around the world revered men who were strong, higher in status and courageous. Mead's "negative instances" caused a sensation precisely because they seemed to be exceptions to a general rule.

dancing them still. Only recently have we begun to discover the invisible cords which have moved us for so long, to feel their silent tugs at our fantasies, judgments, and fears. One can only dimly imagine what the world would be like if we could somehow turn the music off, cut the cords of sex roles, and discover ourselves."[28]

This "mock the poor, misguided, obsolete, insecure straw man" strategy has become the standard tactic of the pro-feminist men's movement. Feminist Tony Doupkil, in his second man-baiting piece for *Newsweek*, referred to modern men as "Beached White Males."

"As if middle age isn't bad enough. The moribund metabolism. The purple pill that keeps your food down. The blue pill that keeps another part of your anatomy up. Now you can't get an effing job? Stuck in your own personal Detroit of the soul, with the grinding stress of enforced idleness. The wife who doesn't look at you quite the same way. The poignantly forgiving sons. The stain on your masculinity for becoming the bread-loser. The night sweats and dark refuge of Internet porn. The gnawing fear that this may be the beginning of a slow, shaming crawl to early Social Security."[29]

Over thirty years after Brannon, male feminists still can't manage to do much more than point and laugh at their own snide caricatures of men, and recommend that men abandon the "musty script of masculinity."[30] Talk about a bunch of guys who are stuck singing the same tune. And, when presented with new, post-Margaret Mead era evidence from evolutionary biologists,

---

28   David, Deborah S., and Robert Brannon, eds. *The Forty-Nine Percent Majority : The Male Sex Role.* Philippines: Addison-Wesley Publishing Company, 1976. 42. Print.

29   Doupkil, Tony. "Dead Suit Walking." *Newsweek* 17 Apr. 2011. Web. 29 Apr. 2011. http://www.newsweek.com/2011/04/17/dead-suit-walking.html

30   Romano, Andrew, and Tony Doupkil. "Men's Lib." *Newsweek.* 20 Sept. 2010. Web. 24 Feb. 2011. http://www.newsweek.com/2010/09/20/why-we-need-to-reimagine-masculinity.html

that tune sounds a lot like "Nyah, nyah nyah, nyah, I Can't Hear You." When Michael Kimmel was asked by *The New York Times* to discuss innate differences between the sexes recently, he dismissed the subject completely and said, "That ship has sailed — it's a done deal."[31]

Kimmel came up with his own knock off of Brannon's list—called "The Guy Code"—for his 2009 book *Guyland*.

Kimmel's "Guy Code" (2009)[32]

"Boys Don't Cry"
"It's Better to be Mad than Sad"
"Don't Get Mad—Get Even"
"Take It Like a Man"
"He Who has the Most Toys When he Dies, Wins"
"Just Do It," or "Ride or Die"
"Size Matters"
"I Don't Stop to Ask for Directions"
"Nice Guys Finish Last"
"It's All Good"

Like Brannon, Kimmel came up with a list of "current epigrams" that presented basic male concerns about status, strength, courage, and competency as a handful of goofy frat boy clichés that he could easily take apart for his readers. Kimmel's straw man was the "guy," an overgrown boy who is obsessed with things that really don't matter. At least, they don't matter to Kimmel and the frustrated young women who would prefer that the young "guys" were obsessed with well-paying careers, nesting, marriage, and starting a (feminist) family.

Kimmel mocked his frat boy students who, despite their apparent

---

31   McGrath, Charles. "The Study of Man (or Males)." *The New York Times* 7 Jan. 2011. Web. 29 Apr. 2011. http://www.nytimes.com/2011/01/09/education/09men-t.html

32   Kimmel, Michael. *Guyland*. 2008. HarperCollins e-books. Kindle. Loc. 902.

ineptitude, manage to keep thwarting his "you-can-have-it-all" feminist supermoms of tomorrow. Brannon's original list has a more patricidal feel to it. Brannon admitted in the "Blueprint" essay that his grandfather was a "rough-and-ready" frontiersman known for killing lawbreakers, and his father was a football star and lumberman. He then described himself as being an absent-minded 90-pound weakling, who tried but failed to be a man according to the standards of his peers and the men in his family.

Brannon's list is clearly a list of his father's values, phrased in the words that men of his father's generation would have used. His slogans were selected to smack the "daddy doesn't love me" button and stir up feelings of resentment and insecurity in his readers. *The Forty-Nine Percent Majority* is itself a collection of essays thick with the jealous, adolescent, Vietnam-era John Wayne-baiting so typical of spoiled, petulant baby-boomers. Brannon's feminism is a passive-aggressive critique of his father's masculinity and the masculine idols of a greater generation. His critical parody of mid-20th century American manhood and his dissection of its contradictions is in part an attempt to one-up his mocking peers and disapproving ancestors.

Yukio Mishima, who also wrote about being a weakling as a young man, had this to say about men like Brannon:

> "The cynicism that regards hero worship as comical is always shadowed by a sense of physical inferiority."[33]

While this is not true of all male feminists (Jackson Katz advertises himself as a former "all-star football player") it is apparently true of both Kimmel and Brannon, and their work continues to be extremely influential in the field of men's studies.

This drive to castrate and discredit the hero-alpha-father is an

33   Mishima, Yukio. *Sun and Steel.* 1970. Trans. John Bester. Kodansha International, 2003. 41. Print.

abstract attempt by low-status males to increase or regain status via intellectual means. The sensitive, bookish outcast screams "Your manhood is false, and you are a fraud!" and then runs into the arms of sympathetic women who tend his emotional wounds and deftly exploit his exposed vulnerabilities, or into a ghetto of other outcast men.

The outcast, omega, or low status male who abandons "The Guy Code" and the "themes" of masculinity idolizes women because fiery women are the foils of alphas. In his telling tale about his father, Brannon was quick to point out that his mother scorned his father for not being a "real man" after he failed to kick her door down during a late-night quarrel.

This vindictive attraction to strong women and castrating bitch-goddesses finds its ultimate expression in gay camp. Gay writer Daniel Harris described gay diva worship as a "bone-crushing spectator sport in which one watches the triumph of feminine wiles over masculine wills," and divas themselves as a "therapeutic corrective [to gay men's own] highly compromised masculinity."[34]

The pro-feminist men's movement has much in common with the gay movement, and the two have been allied since the 1970s. Kimmel seems to have sought the approval of feminist superstars like Gloria Steinem every bit as much as the gay males of his generation wanted to reach out and touch Diana Ross' hand. The intellectual one-upmanship of feminist males has an analog in gay men's fussy bourgeois "aestheticism of maladjustment."[35] Together, they mounted a vengeful evisceration of the ineloquent, brawny philistines who gave them wedgies and made them feel

---

34   Harris, Daniel. *The Rise and Fall of Gay Culture*. Ballantine Publishing Group, 1997. 13. Print.

35   Ibid. 10, 26.

like little bitches.[36]

This "argument from failure" was one of the three main arguments advanced repeatedly against "our culture's positive proscription for masculinity" in *The Forty-Nine Percent Majority*. Brannon wrote:

> "No one less than Attila the Hun could have lived up to that role all the time; we were all losers. But we believed in the values and norms that made us losers, we reinforced them, and we imposed them on others."

Brannon was essentially saying that, because no man embodies all of the manly virtues all the time, all men are failures at being men, so men should stop wounding themselves and each other by holding up an impossible ideal. This argument assumes that the costs incurred by men in failing to embody an impossible ideal are always greater than the total benefits accrued as a result of men striving to prove their manhood. There's no real way to measure these abstract profits and losses. At any rate, evaluating the data will always lead us back to the question: "what is good?" Is the tale of a great hero worth a thousand broken, jealous hearts? Are men better for this collective striving than they would be otherwise?

The argument from failure is, to some extent, an example of the "perfect solution fallacy," in which the "perfect" is made the enemy of the "good." The argument from failure presupposes that for a role to be good, someone somewhere has to be able to live up to that role all the time. It's a little like telling Christians they shouldn't bother trying to be more Christ-like, because they

---

36   David, Deborah S., and Robert Brannon, eds. *The Forty-Nine Percent Majority : The Male Sex Role.* Philippines: Addison-Wesley Publishing Company, 1976. 66. Print. (The Forty-Nine Percent Majority contains a chapter on "Homophobia Among Men," and its author, Gregory K. Lehne continues to specialize in "Evaluation and treatment of sexual and gender identity concerns in children, adolescents and adults. Research and theory on the nature of human sexuality, lovemaps, sexual orientations and gender identities." http://www. hopkinsmedicine.org/psychiatry/expert_team/faculty/L/Lehne.html

will never actually be Christ. For Christians, Christ is a perfect Form in the Platonic sense. He is the embodiment of what they've identified as ideal qualities. The do not expect to become Christ, but feel that by imitating him as best they can, they become better people. One may agree or disagree with the values that they attribute to Christ, or disbelieve in Christ, but the basic concept of bettering oneself through imperfect imitation is what matters here, because men are essentially imitating what they believe to be the perfect Form of Man. All men accumulate a tally of "sins," shortcomings, and near-misses. Feelings get hurt along the way because all men are not equally able to imitate this perfect Form. These facts are not valid criticisms of the manly virtues themselves.

We could call this "The Fallacy of the Impossible Form."

These manly virtues should be considered in their own right, not dismissed because no man can be the complete embodiment of masculine ideals every single day of his life.

Is it better for a man to be "open" or circumspect?

Is it better for a man to be "vulnerable" or invulnerable?

Is it better for a man to have high group status or low group status?

Is it better for a man to be successful or unsuccessful?

Is it better for a man to be tough or delicate?

Is it better for a man to be confident or apprehensive?

Is it better for a man to be self-reliant or dependent?

Is it better for a man to be aggressive or passive?

Is it better for a man to be violent or non-violent?

Is it better for a man to be daring or fearful?

Each of these questions can be asked independently, and the "best" answers will vary according to one's philosophical disposition and the situation at hand. We could speak in Yoda sensei-voices and come up with unexpected, ponderous answers. We could cite exceptions to general rules and instances of "too much of a good thing." But if we refer back to the list of predictions for male mammals in which selection is greater on males, we will see that many of these manly virtues are associated with biological differences between the sexes, and "our culture's positive prescription for masculinity" encourages behaviors that have helped men compete successfully against other men. Our inherited masculine ideal is the stern but sound advice of our forefathers. It is "nurture" working in harmony with "nature."

The second argument made against the male sex role as caricatured by Brannon was that this advice was no longer sound—the argument that "manliness is no longer necessary." There is something to this argument. Philosopher Nassim Nicholas Taleb recently wrote that, "The opposite of manliness isn't cowardice; it's technology."[37]

The Forty-Nine Percent Majority contains an essay by sociologist John H. Gagnon titled "Physical Strength, Once of Significance." Gagnon argued that while the sporting games of boys still produce social hierarchies based on physical strength and prowess, in adulthood, physical strength and prowess have little economic value due to advances in technology. This is probably even truer now than it was in 1976. Having spent five years carrying treadmills and dumbbells upstairs into the home gyms

---

37   Taleb, Nassim Nicholas. *The Bed of Procrustes: Philosophical and Practical Aphorisms.* Random House, 2010. Kindle. Loc. 163.

of the wealthy—so that they could "get into shape"—I am well aware that hard labor doesn't pay as well as neurosurgery.

Gagnon argued that in complex industrialized nations, strength does not justify patriarchal hierarchies as convincingly as it used to. The "cerebral quality" of modern warfare, he imagined, was exemplified Kubrick's mad cripple, Dr. Strangelove. This was a bit of an overstatement. Modern warfare is still extremely physically demanding. Soldiers often have to carry their powerful automatic weapons over difficult terrain. The "'state vs. guerilla insurgent or terrorist" style of current conflicts makes a near future of button-pushing warfare seem unlikely.

In First World "knowledge economies," it is true overall that the martial virtues (virtus, to the early Romans) of our ancestors can handicap a man. Defending your honor will probably land you in prison. Men find themselves doing time for fistfights, let alone duels. Few men make a decent living from physical labor. Even industries like construction are so highly regulated and carefully managed by lawyers and insurance companies that daring applications of strength and agility are discouraged, and the star employees wear back braces and bright orange vests that read "SAFETY FIRST."

This is the world we live in, though it is also true that wealthy nations rely heavily on the risky, back-breaking work of men who live in poorer countries. Still, we should be careful about confusing "modern" with "better" or "permanent." Is our contemporary arrangement better? If so, for whom? Cui bono? Is it permanent? Will things always be so? Will men never need to be strong or courageous again? If we abandon the manly virtues that have characterized the male sex role for all of human history, who will volunteer to risk his life to protect us from the men who have not abandoned those virtues? While it is human nature for men, or at least a portion of them, to desire conflict and risk, will they take those risks if they are despised for it—if all we offer them is a paycheck? Do men watch television shows about the few men left who do dangerous and dirty jobs out of mere curiosity, or because they secretly hate their own weakness and their child-proofed, predictable lives, and fantasize about doing something where their actions have meaningful and immediate consequences?

The third main argument against the traditional male sex role is that "masculinity causes unacceptable collateral damage." Pro-feminist males, being feminists, are primarily concerned with how females have been hurt, subjugated, or inconvenienced by patriarchal social structures. Women, for the most part, gain very little as the result of violent conflicts between men, and have much to lose. Men do gain status, bragging rights, and, at least in the old days, various sorts of booty. Women stand to lose their means of support and protection, and, at least in the old days, were at risk of being raped, abducted, and impregnated by a new "husband."

And yet, women have often clamored for war, because there is something to be said for belonging to a group of victorious, high-status men. There was, for instance, the "white feather" movement during World War I. Women in Britain handed out white feathers—symbolizing cowardice—to men who were not in uniform, and this was hardly the first time or last time that women goaded men into war. More recently, many American women demanded vengeance for the destruction of the World Trade Center on September 11th, 2001. At the interpersonal level, most men are familiar with the scenario wherein a woman "writes a check that he'll have to cash." Some women are known to provoke conflicts between men by casually throwing around fighting words, insults, and challenges—precisely because they won't be the ones expected to do the fighting. Women can usually trash talk with impunity.

Although women sometimes stir up trouble, it is true that

women and children have often been the victims of wars and conflicts that they didn't start or want at all. This is, admittedly, unfair—especially if you believe that the sexes are basically interchangeable and what is good for the goose is good for the gander. If you see males and females as two slightly different kinds of human animals with competing reproductive strategies, then "fairness" and "equality" are impossible goals. Instead of trying to impose an absolute equality of apples and oranges, the question then becomes, "how fair is fair enough?"

It is also frequently argued that men themselves become the collateral damage of their own aggressive status-seeking, but this line of thinking returns us to the argument from failure above.

For all their talk, I doubt that people truly want fairness, equality or "peace." Strategies said to put peace and equality within our grasp invariably end up moving the axe of violent coercion from the hands of one group into the hands of another. This—not "equality" —has been the achievement of feminism. For the first time in history, at least on this scale, women wield the axe of the state over men.

The authors of *The Forty-Nine Percent Majority* explicitly believed that women would be better suited to rule until men were cured of their masculine ailment and liberated from the penal code of the male sex role. While they and their intellectual heirs positioned themselves as experts exploring a new field of study, theirs was not an expedition in search of truth. They were feminist partisans from the get-go, and their caricatured misrepresentations of masculinity were propaganda designed to defame men, trivialize masculinity, and valorize women. Often, their basic assumptions about the flexibility of sex roles and human nature were based on discredited or biased anthropology. Sometimes, their work was clearly intellectual payback for being made to feel inadequate in the world of men. Their primary arguments against traditional models of masculinity are subjective, fallacious, and one-sided. Their conclusions are at odds with human nature, the conclusions of evolutionary biologists, and a cross-cultural assessment of masculine ideals throughout history.

When and where have the majority of men not wanted to be known for strength, daring, and success?

When and where have they been completely unconcerned with their status among other men?

When and where have they wanted to be known as "sissies"?

Any answers will inevitably be desperate references to groups of men who are rare, separate, and exceptional.

Brannon got some of the basic themes of masculinity right, but they are not "American" themes, and they are not tied to a particular time or place. They can be isolated from the skewed noise of his presentation and universalized.

A man's status as a man, his masculine identity—his honor—has been so critical to his sense of self-worth that throughout human history innumerable men and women have worked to shape the "Form" of masculinity to reflect their interests and values. Manly pride can be a man's greatest asset and his greatest weakness. People use a man's sense of himself to manipulate him. Sometimes "man up" simply means "do what I want."

The likes of Brannon play an interesting game. They know that men are concerned with their reputations as men. They know that men want to be seen as strong, so they taunt them and tell them that it is their desire for strength that makes them weak. The reimaginers tell men to reimagine strength.

Is either abandoning his concern with strength or reimagining strength in a man's best interest?

It depends on the man and the context. The answer is philosophical, subjective, and uncertain. What is certain is that by abandoning his concern with strength or by reimagining strength he will be serving the interests of those who ask him to change.

FOREIGN TRANSLATIONS OF THE WAY OF MEN

Der Weg der Männer. (German).
2016. Verlag Antaios. 978-3-944422-24-4

La Voie Virile (French).
2014. La Retour aux Sources. 978-2-35512-061-9

O Código dos Homens. (Portuguese).
2015. Simonsen. 8569041012

Droga Mężczyzn. (Polish)
2019. Czerwona Pigułka 978-83-955612-1-4

El Camino De Los Hombres. (Spanish)
2020. Pan Criollismo.

La Via Degli Uomini. (Italian)
2020. Passaggio Al Bosco. 978-8885574281

La Voie des Hommes. (French - New Translation)
2022. Culture & Racines. 978-2-491861-25-4.

MORE BOOKS FROM JACK DONOVAN

A Sky Without Eagles (2014) ISBN-13: 978-0985452346

Becoming a Barbarian (2016) ISBN-13: 978-0985452353

A More Complete Beast (2018) ISBN-13: 978-0985452377

Fire in the Dark (2021) ISBN-13: 978-0985452384

CPSIA information can be obtained
at www.ICGtesting.com
Printed in the USA
LVHW052034220723
753131LV00036B/1055/J

9 780578 824000